DESK 84- 01215

355.023 Marrs, Texe W.
MA

You and the Armed
Forces

68963

DATE			

DESK

YOU
AND THE
ARMED
FORCES

Texe W. Marrs

ARCO PUBLISHING, INC.
NEW YORK

Acknowledgment

We wish to express our thanks to the Department of Defense for supplying us with the photographs in this book depicting the different aspects of military life.

First Edition, First Printing, 1983

Published by Arco Publishing, Inc.
215 Park Avenue South, New York, N.Y. 10003

Copyright © 1983 by Texe W. Marrs

Library of Congress Cataloging in Publication Data

Marrs, Texe W.
    You and the Armed Forces.

    Includes index.
    1. United States—Armed Forces—Vocational
guidance.   I. Title.
UB323.M29   1983   355′.0023′73   82-16386
ISBN 0-668-05685-1 (Reference Text)
ISBN 0-668-05693-2 (Paper Edition)

Printed in the United States of America

Contents

Acknowledgments

I wish to express my profound appreciation to the many servicemen and women who assisted me in writing this book. The willingness of ROTC personnel and military recruiters to discuss their jobs and their thoughts about the opportunities offered by their services is particularly appreciated.

The recruiters of all four services stationed in Austin, Texas, and the Coast Guard recruiters in San Antonio, Texas, deserve a special note of thanks. They took the time to patiently answer my many questions and provided many of the brochures, manuals, and guides from which information was extracted for use in this book.

I am also grateful to two Department of Defense publications. First, *Profile* magazine, which provided invaluable information about military career specialties and training. A thanks also for the outstanding articles in *SAM* magazine. They gave me unique perspectives on some of the more important issues facing young people in the military services.

I wish especially to recognize Ms. Betty Sprigg of the Pentagon's Audio-visual Office, Washington, D.C., for all her support. She furnished the photographs for the book and also assisted in preparation of the illustrations.

My appreciation also to the personnel assigned to the public affairs offices of the various services. These fine people never hesitated to provide me with the information required to ensure that this book presents an unbiased view of military life.

Many active-duty military personnel of the several services gave me advice on what service life is "really like" and critiqued portions of the book. Again, my thanks.

Finally, my thanks to my editor at Arco Publishing, Ellen Lichtenstein, who recognized that young men and women need a book of good advice and helpful information about the military service and who kindly assisted me in having the book published in a useful format.

Texe W. Marrs
Austin, Texas

1. Get All The Facts

"Should I join the service?" In my job as an Air Force career counselor, I was asked this question repeatedly by anxious young people faced with the choice of whether or not to enter military service. Invariably, my answer to them was, "Get all the facts, then make a decision that's best for *your* life."

No one can tell you whether or not you should join the service; only you can make that important decision. After all, you're the one who will have to spend the two, three, or more years of your life in uniform if you decide to serve your country as a part of its armed forces. What I have done in this book is to provide you with the facts necessary for making a wise decision. Opportunities in the armed forces are numerous, but the obligations and demands of the military upon the individual cause many to decide against going into the service. Described in the following chapters are many of these opportunities as well as the obligations and demands.

There are many reasons why you should consider the military. The service offers advantages such as achieving physical fitness, meaningful employment, economic security, education and training, job experience, and a variety of broadening experiences including travel, adventure, and friendships. But the military also demands sacrifice, hardship, frequent separations from family, constant relocations, the requirement to be on call 24 hours a day, the strictures of military discipline and, not least, the inherent dangers of military operations. All of these liabilities are the price servicepeople pay in exchange for the opportunities the military provides. Indeed, they may be a small price to pay because it is through the sacrifices and dedication of people in uniform that Americans enjoy the freedoms, liberties, and economic well-being of contemporary American society.

In my opinion, the concrete advantages of the military far outweigh the disadvantages, but in the final analysis the choice of whether or not an individual should enter the military profession is a highly personal one. Anyone considering military life should understand the involvements before signing up at the recruiter's office.

This book will tell you what military life is "really like" and what you can reasonably expect in terms of job assignments, promotion and advancement, training possibilities, pay and benefits, and a great number of other matters. It will provide you with an unvarnished and objective view, neither merely extolling all the virtues of a military career, nor discouraging you from enlisting or seeking an officer commission. A balanced perspective is vital in making your decision. Consider, if you will, the person who relies *totally* on a military recruiter for information.

RELYING ONLY ON SERVICE RECRUITERS

Surprisingly, it is next to impossible to obtain from the services all the information you need to know to prepare for military service. Military recruiters are more than willing to inundate you with leaflets and pamphlets that do provide useful data and information. But it is best to keep in mind that these publications, while truthful, are written from the perspective of the service that prepares them. For instance, a Marine recruiter and his publications will tell you his service is superior, that only it has the answer to your future. However, you will get the same pitch from the Air Force, Navy, Army, and Coast Guard recruiters. All recruiters are trained to sell their own service and they undoubtedly believe in what they say. Pity the bewildered young person, though, who spends hours visiting with a recruiter from each of the five services, is given a hundred or so recruiting brochures to read and digest, and is then expected to make a rational decision based on everything he has heard and read.

RELYING ON SERVICE VETERANS

Many persons interested in the military seek information from a friend or relative who is a military veteran. "What is service life really like?" they will ask. "What can I expect?" Even when the friend or relative sincerely wishes to help, their responses can be misleading. For example, a decade ago—when Uncle Joe was in the Air Force—conditions were a lot different than they are today. If he was in the service during the Korean or Vietnam wars, it should be realized that the military has drastically changed from what it was during those eras.

Millions of Americans have served their country in uniform—and served it well—but the conditions you will face and the opportunities that await you are far different than the ones encountered by those who served before you. The thing for you to do, then, is *get all the facts*. First, study this book, then, make an appointment to visit with the military recruiter of the service of your choice. The recruiter will be so impressed by the breadth of your knowledge, your eagerness to learn, and your demonstrated interest in the military that the recruiter probably will go out of his way to make sure you get what you want when you enlist—if you decide to enlist. There again, this book can be your primary tool to make that vital decision of life-long importance.

2. Is Military Life For You?

This chapter is probably the most crucial in this book. Is service life for you? The following discussion, and especially the personal test provided, will help you evaluate your military potential and answer this most important question.

Military life isn't for everyone. During World War II and in the post-war period, when the involuntary draft was in operation, Uncle Sam pretended otherwise. In those days, the need for military manpower was so great that anyone and everyone was considered prime military material. Naturally, there were mental and physical standards a man had to meet. But beyond these minimal qualifications, the message of the U.S. government was that any young man could be taken out of the civilian environment and "made" into a soldier, Marine, sailor, or airman. "Don't worry, boy," the saying went, "we'll mold you into what we want you to be."

The advent of the all-volunteer military force in 1972 changed all this. No longer does Uncle Sam yank someone from civilian life and try to mold the individual into a military cog against his will. Instead, the individual must now decide if service life is his "cup of tea."

ARE YOU MILITARY MATERIAL?

A person needs certain qualities, motivations, abilities, and aptitudes to be a success in the military. Do you have these attributes? To find out, I have designed a series of questions which I call the "Are You Military Material?" test. The questions and answers for the test are based on a survey of active-duty military superiors—officers and NCOs. I asked these career servicepeople, "What working qualities and personality traits do you find most important in a new service-person?" The test below includes the most-mentioned items. How you answer each of the questions in this test is important. Your response should reveal to you whether the military is going to be, for you, a wonderful, action-packed and satisfying adventure or, on the contrary, if your life in uniform would be pure drudgery, bordering on slavery. Are you ready for the test? Let's go!

The Test

Instructions: Answer each of the questions below, carefully considering each of the responses given. Record your choice by checking the appropriate block. At the end of the test there is an explanation of how to grade yourself.

1. Can you cheerfully and willingly follow orders and instructions?
   - ____ (a) Yes, no problem.
   - ____ (b) Usually.
   - ____ (c) It depends.
   - ____ (d) No.

2. Can you accept criticism?
   - ____ (a) Sure.
   - ____ (b) Yes, but I don't like it.
   - ____ (c) Sometimes.
   - ____ (d) No way!

3. Can you be depended on to be on time for work and appointments?
   - ____ (a) Yes, always.
   - ____ (b) Almost always.
   - ____ (c) Sometimes.
   - ____ (d) Hardly at all.

4. Can you pay attention to details?
   - ____ (a) Yes.
   - ____ (b) Yes, but sometimes I slip.
   - ____ (c) If I'm interested.
   - ____ (d) No, who cares about picky details?

5. Can you discipline yourself to learn something new?
   - ____ (a) Yes, I love new challenges.
   - ____ (b) Yes, if necessary.
   - ____ (c) Well, okay, but I prefer the old.
   - ____ (d) No, why change?

6. Can you adjust to being away from home?
   - ____ (a) Yes, I love to travel.
   - ____ (b) Yes, if I have to.
   - ____ (c) Yes, if it's not *too* far from home or for *too* long.
   - ____ (d) No, I'm a real "homebody."

7. Can you work well with others?
   - ____ (a) Yes, no problem.
   - ____ (b) Yes, but I prefer to work independently.
   - ____ (c) Yes, *if* I *like* the others.
   - ____ (d) No, I like to work alone.

8. Can you adjust to working long, erratic and unpredictable hours?
   - ____ (a) Yes, I have a lot of energy.
   - ____ (b) Yes, but I prefer a regular workweek.
   - ____ (c) I can, but my boss must have a good reason for it.
   - ____ (d) No, I'm a 9–5 person and I value my free time.

9. Are you physically fit?
   - ____ (a) Yes, I'm in top shape.
   - ____ (b) Yes, I'm in fairly good condition.
   - ____ (c) I could be in better shape.
   - ____ (d) No, not really, and I detest anything "physical."

10. Can you tolerate someone else telling you how to dress and groom yourself?
    - ____ (a) Yes, no problem.
    - ____ (b) Yes, but I don't really like it.
    - ____ (c) Only if it is *absolutely* necessary, and it usually isn't in the military.
    - ____ (d) No, I am an individual.

11. How much do you value your privacy?
    - ____ (a) I am willing to totally sacrifice my privacy.
    - ____ (b) A lot, but I understand that the military has a need to be deeply involved in most aspects of my life.
    - ____ (c) I'm willing to let the military dictate to me "on the job," but they should stay out of my private life.
    - ____ (d) Greatly, and I don't like anyone "nosing" in my business or personal affairs.

12. Are you willing to participate in an armed conflict and, if necessary, to take the life of opposing enemy personnel?
    - ____ (a) Yes.
    - ____ (b) Yes, but reluctantly.
    - ____ (c) Only if *my* life is threatened.
    - ____ (d) No, I don't believe in war.

Grading Yourself

For each (a) answer, give yourself a score of 4; each (b) gets 3 points; (c), two points; and a (d) response nets you 1 point. Total the number of points you earned from all 12 questions and evaluate yourself according to the following aptitude scale.

If you scored:	Then your potential for success in military service is:
44 to 48 points	Outstanding—military life for you will be a breeze.
39 to 43 points	Excellent—the military and you will get along fine.
34 to 38 points	Fair—both you and the service may become irritated and unhappy on occasion.
29 to 33 points	Dubious—you may wish to consider not going into the service.

Test Discussion

Let's go back over the test questions and discuss their meaning.

1. Can you cheerfully and willingly follow orders and instructions?

Unless you checked the first box ("Yes, no problem,") you better reconsider whether you want to join the service. Military regulations and tradition are big on requiring people to obey the orders and instructions of their superiors. If a civilian boss *demands* you put the screw on Widget A *now* and you refuse, you *might* lose your job. If your military superior gives you a similar order and you answer "no"— well, I'm sure you've heard the old expression "the crossbar hotel." That's where you might end up, counting the days until your court-martial sentence is over!

The Purpose of Orders

Actually, in either civilian or military endeavors, carrying out orders has a purpose. Few supervisors care to have an employee work for them who refuses to follow instructions. After all, supervisors usually become supervisors by proving they have the experience and knowledge to lead others in completing the job. That means, if a subordinate thinks he can do better or knows more, and thus refuses to do what his supervisor requests, the subordinate might best look for another career field or for a job where he can be the boss.

It is not demeaning to be required to follow orders. It certainly doesn't hold that, by being required to follow orders, you will be a "slave." Even the members of the White House cabinet have to follow the orders of a superior—the President; reporters must listen to the instructions of their editors; and construction workers must heed the directives of foremen.

Of course, the military is a special situation in that, in times of war and battle, the very lives of the men and women of a unit can be jeopardized by the refusal of a person to obey orders or to carry them out with less than his full effort and capabilities. This is why the armed forces place such a premium on one's ability to follow orders.

2. Can you accept criticism?

If you plan on entering the military, I hope you chose (a) or (b) for the second answer. Either is fine. You *can* expect criticism of your performance in uniform. Usually this will be in the form of constructive criticism, designed to help you become a fully productive and efficient member of your military unit. Sometimes, however, you may not agree with the criticism made by your superior. It can be tough to stand or sit there and let someone tell you they don't like something about your behavior or appearance when you think the points being made are unfair and, perhaps, inaccurate. In the military, you do have the right to defend yourself from unjust criticism—as long as you use politeness and diplomacy. If you do not agree with the criticism, and you feel strongly about it, you also have the right to go to your critic's immediate superior and state your case.

3. Can you be depended on to be on time for work and appointments?

There's an old joke that asks the question, "What if they called a war and no one showed up?" No answer is given for the joke, but in the real-life military, the answer would be plain—a lot of people would be in a "heap of trouble." The one thing (other than failure to obey orders) most military supervisors detest the most is a person who is chronically late to work or who fails to show up for duty at all.

This strict military attitude also extends to appointments a soldier, seaman, airman, or Marine might have on post. Missing a scheduled appointment with a post, base or ship doctor, a lawyer, dentist, or personnel officer can get you in hot water. Dependability and reliability are character traits greatly respected—and demanded—in the armed forces.

4. Can you pay attention to details?

The services need people who can pay attention to details. Naturally, you may sometimes slip up and details escape your attention. But, generally, the ability to take pains to be exact can be a blessing and an aid to a military career.

The Military Mission

Why should attention to detail be such a "big deal"? Well, consider the type of missions the military services have and the equipment they have to carry out those missions. If you are a munitions handler and you fail to adjust a certain bomb valve to just the right specification, imagine the consequences; or perhaps you are an aircraft mechanic and you fail to use a detailed checklist to inspect your airplane before it is flown away to combat. There are a multitude of other examples:

—You are an artillery specialist, but you fail to adjust the sights on the 101 Howitzer artillery piece. "Goodbye, friendly town!"

—You are a navigator on a naval vessel and your navigational math is a "little" off. "Seaman, why are we in the Barbados Islands when we are supposed to be in Canadian waters?"

—You are a computer programmer at the Air Force's Military Pay Center and you "misprogram" the pay computer. "Hey Sarge, my paycheck is for $3 million this time!"

—You are a tank gunner and you aren't too careful about adjusting the sight to the tank's big gun. "Congratulations, soldier! You just demolished the commanding officer's headquarters building!"

I am sure you can imagine other disastrous scenarios. So if you feel that being precise is just too much bother, then maybe you shouldn't bother volunteering to serve in uniform.

5. Can you discipline yourself to learn something new?

The military services are constantly making changes in every facet of their operations. The old saying, "There are only two things for sure in this world, death and taxes," really needs revision. Change also is assured in almost any field of human activity, and the military is no exception. Often the military is at the vanguard of change.

The Army no longer uses the horse cavalry, the Air Force has few propeller-type airplanes, the Navy has retired the battleship, and even the Marines have changed—some Marines now actually fly airplanes! The bazooka has been replaced by laser- and radar-guided anti-tank weapons, satellite communications systems have taken the place of the old World War II walkie-talkies, and there are now "smart" bombs and missiles that guide themselves to the target.

Most people, especially Americans, appreciate change and desire improvements. It can be an exciting thing to help "break in" or learn a new piece of equipment or procedure. In any case, expect change if you opt for military service.

6. Can you adjust to being away from home?

The services have posts and installations throughout the globe. You name the place and there is probably a U.S. military unit there—or there will be one tomorrow. Many young people are afraid to leave home for the first time, and rightly so. There is nothing wrong with loving one's hometown or state and desiring to remain in a familiar location.

Homesickness is Normal

Most young people do suffer pangs of homesickness and regret after they have forsaken the security and comforts of home and embarked on a new life in the service. But most people do adjust to their new surroundings. Often, after a period away from home, young people begin to enjoy the excitement, variety of travel, and the drama of living in another state or country. Those on ships that tour the world may find such travel a real adventure.

Most servicepeople feel privileged to be able to travel, sightsee, and encounter people and places that are only dreamed about by most civilians. For example, in my own 20 years in the Air Force, I traveled—at government expense— throughout Europe (the Netherlands, Italy, France, Germany, Belgium, and Austria) and Asia (Japan, Thailand, and Okinawa). Yet I recall that when I left home for the first time, I was very, very unhappy and dreamed about "the old hometown."

However, some young people who enter the service do so expressly for the purpose of seeing the world, to travel and escape what they consider to be the humdrum and drab everyday existence of their hometown. If you are of like mind, you'll undoubtedly love the service because your dreams will probably come true. (See Chapter 7 for a discussion of where you will be assigned.)

On the other hand, if leaving home is inconceivable to you, well, you don't want military life. Regardless of what your recruiter tells you about where you will be assigned, and even if there's a military base near your home, don't count on it. If you're a Texan or a Floridian, Johnston Island in the Pacific or Tin City, Alaska, are just as possible as a first assignment in San Antonio or Orlando, so be prepared.

7. Can you work well with others?

Supervisors I interviewed felt the quality of working well with others was the single most important factor that was needed for a new military recruit. The success of a military mission is greatly dependent on the degree of teamwork of the members of a unit. Studies have consistently shown that the winning side in battle invariably is the one that has the most cohesion and morale among its people. The military has a special phrase it uses for this attitude and display of cooperative effort and teamwork—*esprit de corps.* It literally means "spirit of the group."

Most military jobs and tasks are accomplished through a collaborative team effort. When you think about it, the very fact that the armed forces are split into different branches demonstrates this joint nature of the military mission. For example, the services are divided into sea, air and space, and ground forces. It's easy to understand how battles—or an entire war—could be lost unless these different types of military units were brought together in a deliberate and highly coordinated, combined effort.

Therefore, if you checked (a) in answering the question "Can you work with others?" you can expect to be a "leg up" on those individuals who enter the service without this ability.

This quality of getting along well with others has important side benefits as well. As any military veteran will tell you, one of the most rewarding aspects of service life is the warm and enduring friendships a person makes. Many such friendships become lifelong relationships, even though the individuals may come from different backgrounds and live across the country from each other. Getting along with and assisting others in a team effort is an excellent way to cement such friendships.

8. Can you adjust to working long, erratic and unpredictable hours?

Military people often have to work incredibly erratic and unpredictable hours; to put it mildly, the 40-hour workweek is not a respected and hallowed military tradition. This is a result of the military's primary mission, which is to defend the United States and its citizens. This mission of national security is one that continues night and day, 365 days a year, including holidays.

However, all this talk of working holidays, weekends and being available 24 hours a day can be misleading. You should not get the impression that military people work 100 hours a week and never have time off to enjoy sports, recreation, and other leisure activities (in addition to an appropriate amount of time to simply "laze around" or "goof off"). Military people *typically* don't work any longer hours than do civilians. That is, the average military worker puts in no more than 40 hours a week.

Your work hours in the service depend, for the most part, on whom you work for and what the manning strength of your unit is. For example, you are assigned as a vehicle repairperson and the vehicle maintenance shop (*garage* in civilian "lingo") is short of mechanics. Let's say that, of six people needed and authorized, only four are assigned. Shortages in authorized personnel are a way of life in some units. In such a case, you might reasonably expect to have to work overtime to get the job done, to get vehicles back on the street. And I should mention that in time of war or national emergency, your work hours may be extended, perhaps for a long duration of time. It is obvious that if the enemy is attacking your home camp, it would be unwise and foolhardy (and impossible, I might add) for you to lay claim to your well-deserved day off.

In summary, you will probably work no more hours in the service than your civilian counterpart, but you may be asked to work longer hours or to perform duties when most civilians are enjoying leisure activities, such as on Sundays and holidays. If you're a 9-to-5 or Monday-to-Friday person, sorry, but service life for you just will not agree.

9. Are you physically fit?

It goes without saying that the armed services are very demanding in terms of physical fitness. This is especially true for the new enlisted recruit or officer trainee. Upon arrival at boot camp, you will be expected to be in at least moderately good condition. Later, in Chapter 9, we'll thoroughly discuss the rigors and curriculum of basic training, or boot camp. But for now, take my word for it—the physical requirements for the new service member can be very taxing on one's energies.

Weight Standards

According to the services, part of being physically fit is to look that way. If you're excessively overweight, you won't be allowed to enlist. If you enlist and gain too much weight while in service, this could be a problem. There is a maximum allowable weight that each service permits its members to reach. If a member exceeds this maximum, he or she is placed in a formal weight-reduction program. The individual is given a reasonable period of time to lose the undesirable number of pounds. If he cannot, the individual is honorably discharged.

Figures 2-1 and 2-2 are the services' (excluding the Coast Guard) current maximum allowable weight standards. Note that the standards vary widely by service.

Generally, the Army standards are strictest, followed by the Air Force and the Navy/Marines, in that order. Keep in mind that these standards change periodically, so don't consider the chart as an absolute, but only as an approximate guide. Phone the recruiter of the service in which you are interested to find out the current standard.

The military is not a career one enters for a life of ease. If your idea of the good life is a "pot" belly, a six-pack, and tons of snacks every night while you're kicking up your feet and watching television, and if you abhor physical activity, think again before seeing your military recruiter. You just might not be service material.

Height	Weight (in pounds)		
(in inches)	Army	Air Force	Navy/Marines
60	141	153	158
61	146	155	163
62	150	158	168
63	155	160	174
64	160	164	179
65	165	169	185
66	170	174	191
67	176	179	197
68	181	184	203
69	186	189	209
70	192	194	215
71	197	199	221
72	203	205	227
73	208	211	233
74	214	218	240
75	220	224	246
76	226	230	253
77	232	236	260
78	238	242	267
79	244	248	273

Weight Standards for Men (maximum allowable weight)
Figure 2-1.

Height	Weight (in pounds)		
(in inches)	Army	Air Force	Navy/Marines
58	113	126	121
59	117	128	123
60	121	130	125
61	125	132	127
62	130	134	130
63	134	136	134
64	138	139	138
65	142	144	142
66	147	148	147
67	151	152	151
68	156	156	156
69	160	161	160
70	165	165	165
71	170	169	170
72	175	174	175

Weight Standards for Women (maximum allowable weight)
Figure 2-2.

10. Can you tolerate someone else telling you how to dress and groom yourself?

If you are contemplating joining the military, you should be prepared from day one to have people (and that means *anyone* who has more rank than you) telling you *what* to wear, *how* to wear it, and how to groom yourself.

The Military Manual on Appearance

Each service has a complete manual that tells a person everything the service requires for a neat and orderly outward appearance. Every person in the service is made acutely aware of the rules and guidelines in the manual. If you violate these rules in any way, you can count on being corrected by someone who outranks you.

The manuals even have drawings and pictures of "model" soldiers. These models tell you exactly how you are to look. The length and width of your moustache, how long the hair can be on the nape of your neck, and the position of your belt buckle to one-sixteenth of an inch—all these instructions and more are included in the manual.

If you wear your hat cocked to the side a bit but the manual says it should be straight up, someone will let you know that this is an audacious and unacceptable transgression. And you can't say you "just didn't know." Ignorance is no excuse. Within just a few days of basic training, your military instructor will teach you the basics of good grooming. Then you're on your own, and expected to be a sharp, well-dressed soldier.

Need I say that bathing regularly, shaving, and having a fresh (and regulation) haircut are definitely required? Also, long hair, bushy or long sideburns, and anything more than a thin and trim moustache are out as far as the military services are concerned. For a while, the Navy allowed beards for shipboard personnel, but no longer. It's no wonder that barber shops are booming businesses on military installations!

Why This Emphasis on Appearance?

In addition to claims that a neat appearance and good grooming are indicative of job performance, the services worry about the "military image." When civilians see people in military uniform who look unkempt and sloppy, they are usually highly disapproving and critical. This public relations aspect of dress and appearance is a legitimate concern for the military.

In an interview with *SAM* magazine, a DOD (Department of Defense) publication for armed forces personnel, Walter Cronkite of CBS television news fame discussed this aspect of the military image:

> Soldiers, sailors, Marines, and airmen are a cross section of American life. The attitude of the general public is determined by the attitude of the military themselves . . . by the demeanor, posture, and appearance of the individual service-person. If they show by their attitude that "I am a member of the Armed Forces and I'm proud of it," then they'll find a much more responsive public.

As a World War II reporter, Cronkite became acutely aware of the need for upholding an impression of the military by civilian society.

Many service members have decided to get out because they consider the stress put on bearing and appearance "Mickey Mouse." But if you think the stress on bearing and appearance is peculiar to the military, look again. Civilian life is not so different—think of all the jobs that require a uniform: police officers, cooks, medical people, bus drivers, and many others. So, if you can't measure up in the military, you may not make a good civilian either.

11.   How much do you value your privacy?

"The service is like an octopus," the young seaman told me. "There's nothing I do that either I don't have to report to the Navy or else the Navy finds out on its own."

The seaman had told me the sad tale of his off-base arrest for drunken driving. When the local police discovered that he was in the military, they reported the incident to the commanding officer of his naval base.

"It's not fair," he complained. "If I were a civilian, the police wouldn't call my boss. Now, I'm in trouble with the Navy for something I did during my own free time—something that has nothing to do with the Navy!"

"We have higher standards than do most civilian firms," explained a Navy attorney, a Lieutenant. "And our people are still in the Navy even when they're off the installation and wearing civilian clothes. You're all the way in or all the way out."

The fact is that the services have first call on an individual's behavior and conduct. Whether on or off duty, the service member must adhere to service guidelines as to what is moral, proper, and correct. You may not agree that this is fair;

you may complain that it violates your right to privacy. Still, it is the military way of life. If you can't live with it, don't join.

12. Are you willing to participate in an armed conflict and, if necessary, take the life of opposing enemy personnel?

The very reason for a military force is to be prepared, if necessary, to defend the nation from enemy attack. As Sir John Hackett states in his book, *The Profession of Arms*, a military person is expected to "get out there and get killed if that's what it takes." Naturally, the reverse side of the coin also applies—that is, to *keep from being killed*, the military person may find it necessary to kill *others*.

This combat function of the soldier, Marine, seaman, and airman is unique in our society. In no other profession or occupation is the individual literally given a license to kill other human beings. This license, symbolized by the uniform worn by the military person, is an awesome responsibility. Only a mentally deranged person would look upon the prospect of combat, and of killing, with relish. On the other hand, most would agree that if they were being attacked by someone bent on killing either them or their families, they would defend themselves.

There are laws that exempt a person who does not believe in taking a human life from military service. Such a person can apply for conscientious-objector status and, even in time of war, will not be called up for military duty. Probably most Americans have some reservations about fighting in wars and perhaps being put into a "kill or be killed" situation. My experience and, I believe, that of many service veterans is that the military needs people who are sensitive to this issue. It is often the case that the military leader who does his best to minimize death and suffering is also the leader who emerges victorious in battle. As the ancient Chinese expert on warfare, Shin Tzu, once said, "Winning a battle with little bloodshed is the highest state of the art of war."

But, aside from the philosophical issues, let's talk about *you* and *your* feelings about combat and battle. Would *you* be willing to kill the enemy in battle if called upon to do so? If you feel, deep inside, that you could not, you should seriously consider whether military service is right for you.

Summing Up: Are You Service Material?

Well, you've taken the test and read the discussion. How about it, are *you* military material? Do *you* have what it takes—the attitude, motivation, and personality characteristics—that add up to success as a uniformed member of your country's armed forces?

A UNIQUE WAY OF LIFE

The military is a unique way of life. The person who enters military service does so knowing full well that he must sacrifice some personal liberties and freedoms for what his country tells him is a noble cause—the defense of his home, family, and nation. The oath of office each entering military member takes represents the commitment the individual makes upon entering military service. The uniform he wears symbolizes that the new military enlistee or officer is a member of an elite group of Americans charged with an awesome and important social responsibility.

The services themselves contend that military service has attributes which equate it to a "calling," and "activity which transcends individual self-interest in favor of a presumed higher good or dedication to a highly esteemed social role." These words come from a Department of Defense memorandum sent to all the services in 1978. The memorandum also clarifies some of the other concerns expressed in this chapter. It states that the member of the military is *not* just another employee, in the traditional sense or under the law.

> . . . military service has attributes which distinguishes it from concepts in the traditional employer–employee relationships. These include: extended tours abroad; availability 24 hours a day; frequent reassignments; separation from family; amenability to military law and discipline; . . . the inherent dangers in military operations; and the inability of the member to resign at will, to strike or to negotiate over working conditions."

YOUR DECISION

If you decide, after taking the test and reading the foregoing, that you are not military material and that service life is just not for you, fine. It's not for everyone, although in time of war your government may decide that it is! However, if you passed the test with at least a moderately good score and now, more than ever, you are convinced that in the military is where you want to be, great! The remainder of this book is devoted to you.

3. Women In The Military

Does the military offer equal opportunity for women? Well, yes and no. It is true that women are much more welcome in the services than ever before, and today there are a great number of women in uniform. Women do all types of work and serve in a wide variety of career fields and skill areas, many that, just a few years ago, were reserved for "men only." But, still, it would not be entirely honest to say that women have equal opportunity with men in the armed forces. However, relatively speaking, great progress has been made in recent years by the services in this area.

Just what is the status of women in uniform? Obviously, if you are female and you're reading this book to see what military life has in store for you, this question is an important one. No one wants to enter a job or any other type of activity where their contributions are not fully appreciated.

Unfortunately, women have often had to hurdle obstacles in our society that men did not and do not encounter. But this has been a problem for all of society and not just within the military. If anything, women have had *greater* opportunity in the military than in practically any civilian career field or job area. In many instances, the armed forces have had the foresight to lead the way in providing equal opportunity for women and recognizing their talents and abilities.

THE TRADITION OF MILITARY WOMEN

Women have been "in" the U.S. military as long as there has been a United States. In 1775, the Continental Congress authorized a nursing corps. The Army was permitted to have one woman allotted for every 100 sick and wounded. Women served during the Revolutionary War, although in an unofficial status. There was Mary McCaully—"Molly Pitcher" she was called—who became a legendary figure when she heroically carried water to cool red-hot cannon barrels. When her husband was wounded, she took his place in the gun crew.

"Molly's" bravery in combat was considered the exception, and throughout our nation's history women have not been permitted to participate in direct combat.

Women served in the military during World War I, but only as nurses. The Navy called them "yeomanettes," the Marine Corps, "marinettes." These terms implied that the women were seen as little or "mini" servicepeople. Florence Nightingale was a proper role model for the woman in uniform, it was decided, *not* Sergeant Fury, combat hero.

During World War II, women really proved what they could do. "Free a Man to Fight" was a recruiting call answered by some 265,000 women. They served in all of the services—Army, Navy, Marines, and Coast Guard. (The Air Force was at that time part of the Army.) Women served worldwide in jobs ranging from communications to gunnery instruction, jobs that sometimes took them into combat areas. Several military nurses serving in the Pacific became prisoners of war in the Philippines and in Guam. Others were victims of enemy attack and lost their lives serving their country.

In 1943, the Women's Air Service Pilots—WASPs—was formed. About 1,000 women flew 77 types of aircraft millions of miles and provided a tremendous service in ferrying cargo and passengers. The WASPs were deactivated at the war's end, but not before they had proven that women were just as capable of flying jobs as were men.

Since World War II, the number of women on active duty has gradually increased year by year. At first, the law limited the amount of women in the armed forces to two percent of military strength. In other words, of 100 people in uniform, only two could be female. This law was later repealed and women began to enter the service in greater numbers. Also, women were eventually allowed to compete for higher rank.

Even though the proposed Equal Rights Amendment to the U.S. Constitution failed to win enactment, it was the impetus in the seventies for a general push by the services to not only increase the representation of women on active duty, but also to improve the way they were used. More jobs were opened to women and opportunities for promotion and job advancement were enhanced.

THE SITUATION TODAY

Today, women have come a long way in achieving full and equal status with men in the armed forces. Note that I'm not claiming they have been given *truly equal* status. Pockets of unfairness and discrimination remain, but things have gotten better. And compared with many of the roadblocks women face in the civilian world, the military compares well as a place where women can be recognized and rewarded for their abilities and their individual efforts. Let's take a look at today's situation.

A Goodly Number

During the 1970s and the 1980s, women have been steadily added to the armed forces. Today, women comprise about nine percent of the total military strength. That's up from only two percent in 1972. Women are also well represented in the officer corps, the upper management arm of the military. Almost eight percent of officers are women.

While these figures could be higher, women can pride themselves that things are getting better. In fact, if it were not for the increased numbers of women, the

U.S. military may have been forced by now to abandon the all-volunteer military and go to a draft. Over the past decade, not enough men have volunteered and so women have taken up the slack. Who says women aren't needed in uniform?

More women join the Air Force and the Army than the other three services. The Army now has 65,000 women, the Air Force boasts 62,000. The Navy has 33,000 women and the Marines have fewer, mainly because of their sea-combat role. The Coast Guard is smaller in numbers of both men and women—being tiny in size compared to giants like the Air Force, Army, and Navy.

Sorry, Ladies . . . No Fighting Here

The services claim that women are treated equally with men in job assignment and promotion policies. In reality, this isn't the case. Women have a much harder time than do men achieving important and meaningful jobs in the military. And promotions to the upper ranks are pretty much reserved for men as well. Recruiters are reluctant to admit this, but it's true.

The fact is that the services don't want a woman as much as they do a man. The reason for this lies not so much in the sex differences, physical or mental, between men and women as in the way that public law treats the *use* of women by the services.

The largest hindrance to effective use of women is that congressional law prohibits the assignment of women to career specialties and jobs in which combat is required. This means, for instance, that women cannot be assigned by the Navy to combat ships, aircraft carriers, and submarines. Yet such vessels constitute the very core of our naval force's fighting ability.

Likewise, the Army is precluded from giving women jobs in such well-respected and vital fields as infantry and tanks. And the Air Force can't let women fly combat aircraft like the ultra-modern F-15 and F-16 or bombers such as the older B-52 and the projected new B-1 and "stealth" bombers. Since the Marines have the deserved reputation of being combat warriors *par excellence*, public law prohibiting women from being assigned to combat duty severely limits job opportunities and career advancement for women Marines.

One critic has stated that restricting women from combat involvement is like telling female employees of AT&T they cannot touch a telephone. This criticism may be a far-fetched analogy, but it does have a slight ring of truth to it. Since combat is the primary reason for the existence of a military force, the exclusion of women from direct conflict in combat means they are relegated to a second-place role.

However, it is hard to fault the military services. After all, it's not their law and they are forced to live with it. As a matter of fact, considering their inability to assign women to combat-type jobs, the military branches have done extremely well in placing women in positions of responsibility. The services have conducted a number of studies on how they can best use women, and they have made steady progress toward minimizing restrictions. Surely, the military deserves a pat on the back for its diligent efforts in this regard. Let's consider what has been achieved.

Recruiting

Several years ago, women really got the short end of the stick when they made their way to the recruiter's office. For one thing, recruiters could only sign up a select few of the women because, unlike male applicants, women who wished to enlist were presented with a number of obstacles. Women had to take their own entrance exam, the Armed Forces Women's Selection Test, generally acknowledged as much more difficult than the male's AFQT test. They had to be interviewed and approved by a female officer and be recommended by their high school principal. But the unfairest requirement of all was what some recruiters called the "No Uglies Test." As incredible as it may seem, until a few years ago one of the unofficial criteria for a woman to enter the military was that she be attractive! Recruiters were required to submit a full-length photograph of the female applicant to headquarters. There, all the female applicants' qualifications were compared—including how physically attractive they were—and a decision was made on which female would be permitted to enlist.

A recruiter friend once confided to me that because women considered unattractive or "homely" seldom were selected, he resorted to sending the otherwise qualified woman applicant to a hair stylist and a designer clothing shop to prepare to have her photograph taken!

Fortunately, good looks are no longer a consideration, but other forms of recruiting discrimination remain. Sadly, most of the services still maintain different (and higher) requirements for women than for men both in the level of educational attainment and the score on the all-important service entrance exam, the ASVAB. The reason for this discrimination lies in the fact that, due to the combat restriction, women are not as easy to assign as are men. But there is another limitation. Congress has set definite limits on how many women can serve on active duty. For example, as of 1982 the Air Force was limited to 65,000 women, or about 12 percent of the total number of airmen on active duty. When the number of women in blue approaches the upper limit of this allowable target, the Air Force is forced to apply the brakes and limit the number of new women recruits. The other services are faced with this same predicament. Unfortunately, the responsibility to discourage and disapprove women applicants falls on the shoulders of the poor, harried military recruiter.

Recruiters are given monthly quotas that they must reach. They must sign up and send to basic training a specified number of persons each month. This quota is sometimes broken down by sex. For instance, Sergeant Joe Smith of the Army's Indianapolis Recruiting Office may be required to fill a quota of, say, 50. But of this 50, 45 must be men and only five can be women. Sometimes, *all 50* must be men!

Now a recruiter is allowed to exceed his recruiting goals. In our theoretical case, if Sergeant Smith's quota is 50, and 45 must be male, he can exceed this by recruiting more than 50 people. But he is in trouble if he doesn't get at least the 50 people, including five women, to sign on the dotted line.

But although Sergeant Smith can sign up as many women as he can qualify, he will be given credit for no more than the *five* women needed to fill his assigned quota. If poor Sergeant Smith is having a hard time finding enough men but has plenty of qualified women, it won't help him a bit. He'll just have to get moving and find more men. If you, the highly qualified female applicant, are unfortunate enough to encounter Sergeant Smith during this time of crisis, he is liable to give you a polite version of the brush-off. Sure, you are eligible to join the service, but he won't receive any credit for you and, meanwhile, his boss is demanding to know why he hasn't met his male recruiting quota.

At that point, no matter how nice and considerate Sergeant Smith is, he may decide that any time he gives a woman is wasted and not wisely spent. "Come back next month, I'm too busy just now," he might tell you as you enter his recruiting office door.

Job Assignment

Women may be assigned to the vast majority of service specialties and career fields with the exception, as stated previously, of those that are combat-related. However, this still leaves open to women a fantastic array of interesting and highly worthwhile jobs.

As we will discuss in Chapter 5, the military offers career- and job-training opportunities that are virtually unparalleled in civilian life. Most offer access to women, including many jobs in skills formerly reserved for males—mechanics, electronics, plumbing, carpentry, heavy-equipment repair, and a multitude of others.

If you qualify and are accepted on active duty, you will have an equal opportunity for the job and the training you want. Naturally, you must meet the minimum requirements for the job or specialty by demonstrating on an exam that you have the aptitude to be a mechanic, police officer, or whatever. In addition, if the job requires brawn and muscle—for example, the lifting of a heavy tool box—you might have to take and successfully pass a physical strength test. But these same requirements exist for males as well, and there is no discrimination against women in their administration.

Military Occupations Open to Women

A rundown of the number of occupations in each service open to women is as follows (Coast Guard figures were not available):

Army.   Women serve in 293 of 354 job areas (83 percent).
Air Force. Women serve in 226 of 230 job areas (98 percent).
Navy.   Women serve in 83 of 99 job areas (84 percent).
Marines.   Women serve in 34 of 38 job areas (89 percent).

What do these figures tell us? Well, for one thing, they point out that women still don't have equal opportunity. But just as important is the fact that women are welcome in most military fields. And compare the percentages with civilian employment. Take the Air Force: 98 percent of its jobs are open to women. You won't find that kind of batting average in the civilian work world.

Promotions

Women in uniform face the same promotion standards as do men. As a woman, you will have the same opportunity as a man to achieve increased rank and responsibility. However, it must be said that in the higher grades lack of direct combat experience and the inability of women to demonstrate their ability to function in a combat environment will hurt their chances for promotion.

It is a recognized fact that the higher military grades—especially in the officer ranks—are pretty much reserved for those who do or may, in time of war, operate and manage the machinery of combat—tanks, planes, ships, and missiles. To the extent that women are excluded from assignment to these jobs, promotion opportunities are limited. This is one reason why the services have only a handful of generals. That's the bad news.

Now the good news. This limitation should not affect you in the least during your first enlistment and your first few years on active duty. If you decide to make it a career and hope someday to be a general, chief of staff of the Army, or the Marine commandant, you might have a hard row to hoe. To get to the top in the military, you need combat experience on your record.

But how many people, male or female, become general anyway? So, for most military grades, it's fair to say that, as a woman, your chances to go up the ladder are just as good as the next person's, even if that next person is a man with a combat skill.

Sexual Harassment

There have sometimes been charges by enlisted women of sexual harassment by their male peers and superiors in the military. This has been acknowledged as a management and human relations problem not only in the military but in many civilian firms as well. Fortunately, in the military few persons succeed in getting away with treating women as sex objects. Sexual harassment is strictly forbidden by all the services. Physical "patting," suggestive language, and threats that a female will suffer job-wise if she doesn't "cooperate" sexually constitute sexual harassment as far as the services are concerned. A promise to "help" the individual by preferential treatment of some sort—in work assignment, duty hours, promotions, or whatever—in return for sexual favors is also against service regulations.

A person who is the target of such harassment has several avenues she can take. The military organizational chain of command allows an individual the right to go directly to the perpetrator's boss and report the incident. If the violator's superior refuses to take appropriate action, the person may take her case to the next higher superior and may continue moving up the chain until justice is done.

In addition, every military person has a commanding officer who can act as an ombudsman, and all enlisted persons have a first sergeant or similar individual charged with overseeing the welfare of persons assigned to the unit. These officials have the power to take action against superiors who wrongly harass their subordinates.

Finally, the incident may be officially reported to the Inspector General (IG) or an Equal Opportunity counselor. Every military installation has individuals appointed to these duties and their power to remedy bad situations is far greater than you might imagine.

In effect, then, sexual harassment happens far less within the military than it does in civilian life. The surest way a male superior can damage his career is to try to take sexual advantage of a female subordinate. So, for that reason, incidents of sexual harassment are rare.

The friction caused by men and women working and living together in close quarters does, however, breed sexual problems and difficulties. Military women sometimes complain that some of their male peers tend to make sexually suggestive remarks and berate women as individuals and workers. This undoubtedly occurs but reflects perhaps more on the general status of male-female relationships in society as a whole than it does on any service inequities or institutional harassment.

Don't assume, however, that because you are a woman you won't be accepted by your male workmates and peers. As long as you do your job or duties well and show you're as deserving as the next person, you'll be accepted for what you are, a valuable member of the service. This acceptance was noted by Brigadier General Joseph P. Franklin, the Commandant of Cadets of the U.S. Military Academy. Quoted in *Army Times* magazine, the general said, "The vast majority of male cadets at West Point accept women cadets. As women proved themselves over the past four years, acceptance has grown."

The situation is the same among the enlisted and officer active-duty forces. Research opinion studies have shown that, by and large, women are accepted. A majority of men now feel that women are an asset to the military.

Geographical Assignment Limitations

In a few unusual instances, women are barred from an assignment due to a lack of facilities for women at that particular military installation. This problem has been resolved at most sites and posts by the building of new facilities or the modification of old ones. Nevertheless, lack of female facilities is often still the basis for not assigning women to small isolated posts.

In addition, there are a few nations in the world who are not as liberated in their ideas and practices toward women as is the United States. In Saudi Arabia, for instance, military women are looked on with disfavor and even disgust. Women in most of the Moslem nations are denied leadership roles of any sort, especially in the military.

So, to prevent any hard feelings or misunderstandings by the citizens or the allied military personnel in those nations which do not respect the role of women in the U.S. military, our government often will not assign American women to posts in these countries. This may seem to be a capitulation to prejudice, but from the perspective of the Saudis and our hosts in other such nations, this policy is perceived as respect and tolerance of their customs and tradition.

However, such geographical limitations are rare and are becoming even more rare. All in all, women are subject to being assigned to the same military bases as are men. Considering the fact that Americans in uniform are stationed in over 100 nations around the globe, you will have a marvelous opportunity as a woman to "see the world" as a member of our armed forces.

If You Become Pregnant

One situation that is unique to servicewomen and that men do not have to encounter is pregnancy. The services have now liberalized the personnel rules concerning pregnancy.

If you become pregnant while on active duty, you will be given from four to six weeks of maternity leave. This time off will not be counted against your regular leave or vacation time. And, of course, your baby can be delivered cost-free at a service hospital. Prenatal and postnatal care are also taken care of by the military medical system.

Military women who deliver a baby may be discharged at their request, but they may stay on if they so desire. All the services have maternity uniforms and it is becoming a common occurrence to see expectant women in uniform performing their military duties.

However, if your job entails heavy labor, your doctor is authorized to have you transferred to lighter duty until after the baby comes and you are again fit for full duty.

A FINAL PERSONAL NOTE TO WOMEN

If you're a woman considering military service, there are two things you should expect. One is to be given a job and training that will match your abilities and allow you to express yourself as a person. It should be a job that makes you feel that you are doing something valuable with your life. The services will offer you such a job on an equal basis with men, except for the few combat-related jobs closed to women.

Second, you should expect fair and equal treatment in that job and, indeed, in all areas of your military life. I believe that generally you'll receive this type of fair, unbiased treatment. On that rare occasion when you do not—when you run into an obstinate person who fails to look past your gender and judges you not as a person but as an inferior "female"—there are things you can do in the military to set things right. Complain to your superior or an Equal Opportunity officer, or even write to your congressman.

Always insist on being treated first-class. That's what you are—first-class—to the military services. They need good women as well as men. A Pentagon study found that women join the service primarily to better themselves. If you want to do something for yourself and your country, join the armed forces!

4. Which Service Is Right For You?

Which one will it be—Army, Air Force, Navy, Marines, or Coast Guard? Each service has its advantages and its disadvantages. Each service plays a vital role in defending our nation from foreign aggression, and has outstanding people and leaders. Which service is right for you?

To answer this, we need to carefully study each of the five services. What is their role and mission? How many people do each have and what do they do? What life-style differences exist among the services?

Maybe you have already decided on one service or the other. For many people, that is one of the first decisions they make. Rarely does a person "comparison-shop" among the services to see which one will give him the best "deal." Maybe someone whom you trust and whose opinion you respect has told you a lot of great things about the Army, the Air Force, or another of the services, and that has convinced you to join that particular branch. Fine. A personal reference can often be a valuable way to gauge the merits of an individual service. Or maybe you've wanted to join one or the other of the services since you were a kid. Perhaps airplanes and missiles engage your interests and make you want to be a part of the Air Force. It could be that the call by the Marines for "a few good men" has made you decide you are one of those few and proud individuals who can contribute to your nation by wearing the Marine uniform. All of these can be compelling reasons why you choose a particular branch of military service.

There are many factors to consider in choosing which service to enter. The enlistment option, opportunities for advancement, job training, and other inducements offered by a service may appear attractive, even irresistible, to you. Usually the choice of service is based on the life-style an individual desires for himself. It is well known, for example, that the Air Force is the most "civilianized" of the services, while the Marines are the most "military-oriented" and traditional.

A few people even decide on a service because they like the uniform of that service. One chap, being told by his girlfriend that Air Force blue brought out and complemented the ice-blue feature of his own eyes, rushed down to the USAF recruiter and signed up as soon as possible! Trusting that you are going to base your own choice on quite a bit more than your favorite uniform color—or someone else's—furnished in this book is a substantial amount of information to help you in your decision.

MORE THAN JUST COMBAT

All of our military services pride themselves on being fully prepared for combat. It stands to reason that a military force that can't fight isn't much of a deterrent to a potential aggressor. But this readiness for combat doesn't mean that the only mission of the services is combat and fighting. The Air Force and the Coast Guard, in particular, are proud of their rescue role, both on land and sea. In fact, all of the services have much to be proud of in the fields of peacekeeping, disaster control, and many other non-combat areas. Similarly, many of the occupations available in the military services are not directly related to combat missions, although everyone in uniform in some way contributes to this combat role.

In choosing the service that is right for you, you may wish to consider the fact that, although a service like the Marines may have a public image of "pure" combat, there are many different occupations held by Marine Corps personnel of a purely support nature. Likewise, not everyone in the Air Force flies planes, as many civilians suppose; not everyone in the Army is a foot soldier; and not everyone in the Navy serves aboard a ship or submarine. That doesn't mean that you won't have the opportunity to do so, if you desire it, but it does mean that all the services are modern, sophisticated fighting organizations. In today's military, computers and satellites are used by the Army, Navy, and Air Force just as much as are the basic weapons systems—rifles, planes, tanks, etc.—that most people connect as the province of one or the other of the services.

Don't underrate any of the services because of a popular misconception about their mission or their life-style. You may find out that your own ambitions and personal goals can be met by a different service than you originally supposed. Approach what the services have to offer with an open mind, *then* make your decision.

SIMILAR JOBS

To underscore this message, I have provided Department of Defense figures on the occupational distribution of service personnel in all the branches except the Coast Guard. See Figure 4-1.

MILITARY OCCUPATIONS DISTRIBUTION

Occupation	Army	Navy	Marine Corps	Air Force
Infantry, armor, and gun crews	23.3	3.7	23.3	6.4
Electronic equipment repair	4.2	13.0	4.4	13.0
Communication/intelligence specialist	9.4	8.3	6.7	7.0
Medical/dental specialist	5.2	5.1	0.0	4.3
Other technical specialists	2.1	1.1	1.7	3.4
Administrative and clerical	15.8	9.7	13.3	21.2
Mechanical equipment repair	14.4	26.5	15.7	22.7
Craftsmen	2.3	5.6	2.6	5.4
Service and supply workers	10.6	5.4	11.1	9.0
Other (including trainees)	12.8	21.4	20.9	7.5
Total (approximately)	100.0	100.0	100.0	100.0

(Numbers shown reflect the percentage of personnel assigned in each occupational area.)

Figure 4-1.

Note in this chart that each of the services has people in practically every occupational area. The Marines have a little over 23 percent of their people in direct combat skills—infantry, armor, and gun crews—but they have even more people working in support fields such as electronic and mechanical equipment repair, communications, and medical. Evidently, not everyone in the Marines is an infantry rifleman.

The chart demonstrates that the *majority* of military occupations are not combat-related. Yet every occupation shown is vital to the mission of our armed forces. The Air Force, for instance, needs pilots, but it also needs mechanics to keep the planes flying, engineers to design and maintain airfields, supply people to order airplane parts, and cooks to feed everyone.

What this means for you is that the occupation or job in which you are most interested may be available in more than one service. You can turn to Chapter 5 for a complete listing of the occupational specialties available in this service. If you find that the job you want is offered by one or more services, then you will be free to look for other reasons or factors to decide whether a particular service is right for you. As you are well aware, even though all of the five services may offer you a job as, say, a computer operator, this doesn't make their job offers equal. There is much more to each service than merely the jobs available.

Now for a discussion of the factors that make each service unique: *role and mission; composition* (people and what they do); and the *life-style* characteristics that make the service distinctive. Let's start with the "baby" of the services, the U.S. Air Force.

THE AIR FORCE

The Air Force is the newest of the services. Created only a generation ago, in 1948 (the Air Force used to be a part of the Army), the Air Force today is our second-largest branch, with 564,000 personnel.

There is a certain charisma about the Air Force. Its role in space and its achievements in technology have given it a certain image that is unlike any of the other services. Because of this, the Air Force has never had the recruiting problems of the other services. More than enough qualified people are now willing to put on Air Force blue!

Role and Mission

The U.S. Air Force has the responsibility of providing aerospace forces to prevent war and to establish air and space superiority in the event of war. The Air Force provides strategic aircraft and missile forces and defends against air and missile attack. In addition, this service is the airlift supplier for all the nation's military services, and has tactical land-based air forces to provide air support of ground troops in combat.

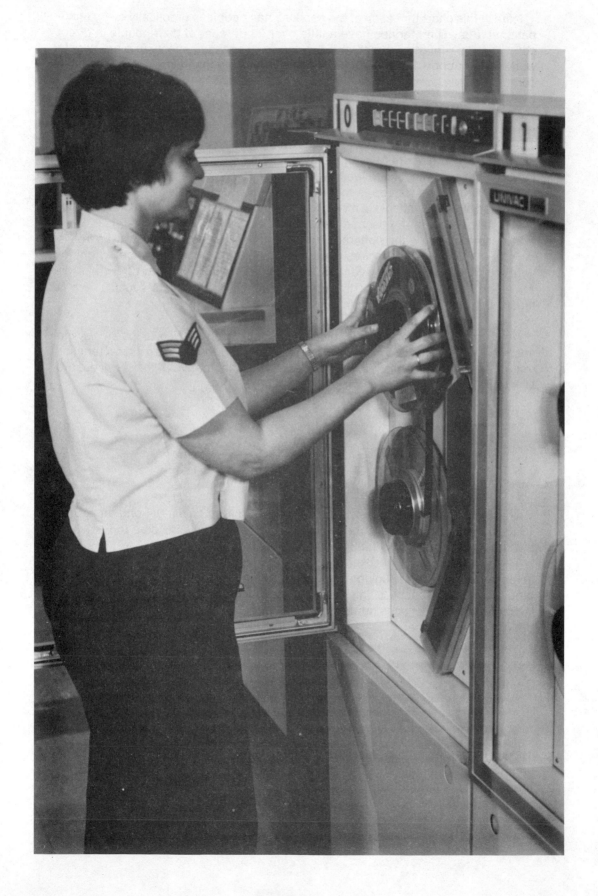

The Air Force provides the major space research and development effort of the Department of Defense. Its work in the areas of lasers, the space shuttle, missiles, satellite systems, and in other highly technological fields makes the Air Force the "glamour" service.

The Air Force has modern fighter aircraft like the F-15 and F-16 based in both the United States and at many overseas bases. Its strategic bombers include the older B-52 and FB-111 now in use, and a new generation (the B-1 and "stealth" bombers) either in production or on the drawing board. And our Air Force is the owner of the world's largest aircraft—the giant C-5A—and has a variety of other cargo aircraft.

There are approximately 1,050 land-based Intercontinental Ballistic Missiles (ICBMs) in the Air Force inventory. A new missile system, called the M-X, is now under development and new, accurate cruise missiles are being used.

The Air Force also has a great quantity of helicopters which it uses for many different roles, including the rescue and recovery of downed pilots and people in distress.

Defense as well as offense is the Air Force's forte. Detection of enemy attack is achieved by use of sophisticated radar and satellites. The Air Warning and Control System (AWACS) aircraft play a role in both defense and offensive capabilities.

The Air Force is known for its flexibility. B-52 bombers can be flown around the world and provided with in-flight refueling. Within a few hours notification, fighter bombers can be in the air and headed for almost any trouble spot in the world. Satellites can pick up evidence of a Soviet missile attack, flash this information to the Strategic Air Command, and the President will be informed within minutes.

Airmen have been extremely successful in combat. The German Luftwaffe was destroyed by a combination of U.S. and British air power and, in the Korean War, U.S. pilots shot down ten Russian-built MIGs (fighter aircrafts) for every American plane downed.

Composition

The Air Force is made up mainly of people in technical skills. Studies have shown that over 85 percent of the occupational skills in the Air Force are transferable to the outside.

The modern Air Force could not run without computers, and there are more officers in scientific, engineering, and technical jobs than there are officers who fly. The Air Force is definitely at the forefront of space exploration. A new Space Command has been set up to handle all space activities and many astronauts come from Air Force pilot ranks. Also, thousands more work in the missile field.

All pilots and navigators are officers, but many enlisted personnel are on flying status, serving as gunners, technicians, loadmasters, air medical specialists, and in a number of other fields related to air operations. However, the majority of enlisted people—and most officers—do not fly.

It is well to keep in mind that while the Air Force is the most technologically oriented of the services, there are still plenty of jobs for people in non-technical fields. The civil engineering branches in the Air Force offer occupations in plumbing, carpentry, electronics, and even street maintenance. There are thousands of supply and administration people in the Air Force blue, plus many airmen in recreation, accounting, parachute rigging, education, and other career fields. It takes people in many diverse areas to operate the best air force in the world.

Life-style

Compared to the military-oriented grind of the other services, the Air Force offers a more relaxed life-style. But the Air Force is definitely a fighting force. Its direct combat forces are chiefly the pilots who fly the planes. Missile personnel also are combat-oriented, but not in the traditional sense. As with pilots, missile operations personnel are exclusively officers. They typically sit far from the actual scene of combat, prepared to turn the keys and unleash the horrible effects of the nuclear weapons mounted on our missiles.

But this does not mean they are not to be involved directly in combat. It is well to keep in mind that merely being on a major air base makes you a prime target in event of war. Air Force installations are priority centers for hostile enemy bombs. Air bases *can* be overrun by enemy ground forces.

Still, being in the Air Force is more like having a civilian 8-to-5 job than is the case in the other services. Except for people in a few career fields, most Air Force personnel are not subjected to physical fitness training, and the old-style military "spit 'n polish" atmosphere.

Rarely do Air Force commanders and supervisors conduct parades, military drill, or dress inspections. Airmen who live in the dormitories generally live the way they want, except for occasional sanitary and health inspection visits by superiors.

Airmen live in two-men or -women rooms in dormitories that are the equal or better of the facilities on most college campuses. They use their own bedspreads, have attractive blinds and curtains on the windows, and are otherwise free to decorate their rooms according to their own individual taste.

Air Force dress standards are probably a little more lenient than those of the other services. Hair on males is expected to be short but certainly not of the "white sidewall" variety. (See the Marine life-style section below!)

All in all, the Air Force emphasizes the job and overall mission accomplishment rather than enforcing a strict military environment.

THE MARINES

The Marines are at the other end of the spectrum. "The Few . . . The Proud," they call themselves. A lot is said of men by Marine recruiters, but little of the female component in this service.

The Marine Corps is much smaller than the Army, Navy, and Air Force, having only 185,000 members. This makes the Marine Corps population only about one-fourth that of the Army.

The Marines are known for their high-spirited ways and traditional military rules of behavior. Their nickname, "Leatherneck," epitomizes the rough-and-ready image they portray and enjoy. Naturally, the Marine Corps has evolved and changed a lot over the past 200 years, since their founding in 1775, but the Marines don't like to admit it.

The Marine Corps emphasizes its combat role. "First to Fight" is one of its mottos. Killing when necessary is recognized as a necessity by Marines, in order to carry out the mission when they are called on.

Role and Mission

The Marines are the United States' amphibious fighting force. They constitute a separate service, yet they are under the topside direction of the Navy.

Traveling with the naval fleet and ready for combat, Marine forces are capable of seizing or defending naval bases and land sites. They are trained to embark from naval vessels and attack land forces from the sea, arriving in specially designed landing craft. The masterful operations carried out by the Marines at Inchon, Korea, and earlier in World War II in the islands of the Pacific, demonstrate just how well this service can carry out its assigned combat role.

Composition

The Marine Corps has people not only in the amphibious infantry role, but has personnel in many other occupational specialties as well. For example, the Marine Corps has air units which serve aboard Navy aircraft carriers, using a variety of aircraft. These include the Harrier vertical take-off and landing jet aircraft. Marines operate tanks and tracked vehicles. The Marines also have the unique mission of guarding the more than 100 U.S. embassies around the world and they are charged with protecting the President when he is at his Camp David retreat. In addition, Marines guard every major naval installation and ship.

As I mentioned previously, Marines are also assigned in a large number of non-combat career fields. These include supply, administration, weather, utilities, electronics, transportation, and medical areas.

Major Marine units operate with the naval fleet in many world trouble spots— those places where conflict can occur with little warning. This includes the waters of the Middle East, the Indian Ocean, and the Western Pacific. A large Marine force is based in the Japan/Okinawa area. Major United States contingents include one in North Carolina and another in California, covering both the East and West coasts.

Life-style

The life-style of Marines depends, to a large extent, on their occupational field and whether or not they are assigned sea duty. Your first assignment will likely be aboard a Navy carrier, cruiser, or other vessel.

Ship life is not nearly as romantic as the movies make it. Life aboard a military ship is not like pleasure cruising on a luxury yacht, by any means! Living quarters are tight, though they suffice. Food is probably better than that offered on shore because the Navy tries to make conditions afloat as amenable as possible. Movies are offered free on ship and there is a modestly stocked library on board in addition to other recreational outlets.

Life ashore, either in the U.S. or abroad, is much like that in the Army, except that there is even more emphasis placed on keeping physically fit, maintaining self-discipline, obedience to orders, and active support of unit morale and pride. Hair is cut extra short and uniforms are immaculate.

Single Marines living on the post or installation have life more difficult than do the members of other services. They do have rooms now, occupied by either two or sometimes four persons, but their rooms have to be maintained in a military order—though not under the boot camp's picayune and pristine conditions.

The Marines have a reputation of being the best combat force found anywhere. If you join this small and elite group, expect a military life-style in keeping with tradition and the tenets of duty, honor, and sacrifice. There's nothing wrong with these tenets, and all the services require such qualities of their people. However, the Marines are not as prone to tolerate laxity in discipline and continual carping about conditions. If you feel you've got it too hard, they say, you *shouldn't* be a Marine, join the Army instead or, better yet, the Air Force.

THE NAVY

The U.S. Navy is more than just a collection of fighting ships with a few assorted submarines, as television and movies have depicted. Few civilians really understand either its mission or its makeup. It is much, much more than you might imagine.

It might surprise you to know that the Navy has almost as many aircraft as the Air Force. Also, the Navy is unique in that it is the only service other than the Air Force to have a strategic, nuclear mission. Also, the Navy has the only nuclear propulsion systems (for its carriers and some submarines). Finally, the notion that the Navy is manned only by laboring sailors who swab decks and captains who man the stern is way out of line. The Navy is second only to the Air Force (some claim it's first) in the number of personnel assigned to technical career fields. It takes the most sophisticated technology available to accomplish the mission of the modern-day U.S. Navy.

Role and Mission

The Navy has over 528,000 personnel assigned. Their mission, simply put, is to control the seas. This is both a defensive and offensive role. The Navy must have sufficient forces to prevent or ward off enemy attack by sea of U.S. property and personnel and to win objectives at sea and abroad as directed. However, simple though this sounds, it is a complex mission.

The U.S. Navy not only must control the seas, it must be able to project U.S. military power around the world. To this end, it has some 450 ships and more than 6,000 aircraft. Its aircraft carriers are unparalleled. The F-18 aircraft—the major weapon system aboard our carriers—is one of the finest fighting aircraft in the world.

The Navy has Polaris-class submarines armed with sea-launch-ballistic missiles (SLBMs), which carry nuclear warheads. The new and massive Trident submarine, three football fields in length, has newer, multiple-targeted SLBMs.

Whenever there is trouble in the world, the Navy is either there or can get there soon with either conventional or nuclear weapons. It can bombard shore targets miles and miles inland with heavy guns or it can launch fighter-bombers against land targets.

Composition

The Navy has people in a large number of career areas. Because ships and naval stations operate as self-sufficient communities, people are needed in almost every occupation: pilots, telephone operators and maintenance, aircraft mechanics, food service, supply, computers, postal, medical, and firefighting. The Navy has some of the best technical schools in the world, to teach sailors the skills they need to run naval installations and operate the modern ships, subs, and airplanes.

Navy ships are deployed in the Mediterranean (the Sixth Fleet, which watches over the vital Middle East region), Atlantic, Pacific, and Indian oceans. Read this list over again and you'll notice that there are Navy vessels everywhere around the globe.

In addition, the navy operates a large establishment of shore stations and training bases.

Life-style

Sea duty! That's what makes the Navy (and Marine) life-style different from that of the other services. Men and women in the Navy have the opportunity to "ride the waves." Women, however, are prohibited from combat vessels, a restriction that significantly limits their chances of sea duty. Naval personnel can expect to be assigned to sea duty their first assignment, though a great many are sent on shore duty their first time around.

Sea duty doesn't mean you'll be at sea 365 days out of the year. Navy ships and submarines have a home port. They sail out of the home port and are away for a total of about six months out of the year. During this six months, they will be at sea

around half the time. Generally, however, two to three weeks is the longest stretch they'll be at sea before berthing. When they berth at a port, there's time for rest, relaxation, and sightseeing. Sometimes repairs are needed on the ship, so you might be busy while it's tied up.

There are no alcoholic beverages allowed while at sea, so if you can't hold out for a while without beer or hard liquor, don't join the Navy!

It is true that the Navy goes out of its way to bring shore life to the sea. On board, there are doctors, movies, libraries, religious services and chaplains, and other means of making oneself at home. But work also awaits the seafarer. You can expect to put in much more than eight hours a day; twelve-hour days are more like it.

Naturally, the quarters aboard ships are cramped, though they're a far sight from the way they used to be on now-antiquated ships. Submarine duty is especially rough. The Navy has trouble getting and keeping people who can withstand the uncommon life of the submarines. Submarine duty is better than ever before; for one thing, the subs are larger and there's more privacy space. Still, underwater is underwater, and a lot of sailors would prefer not to have this duty.

The nicest thing about sea duty for many sailors is the opportunity to travel. Navy people trek all over the world: Europe, the Middle East, Hawaii, and Japan. You name the port and a Navy ship pays a call there.

While your ship or submarine is in home port, you'll still sail out about 10 to 14 days a month for local ocean-going maneuvers and exercises. There'll be training, repair work, and maintenance to be done, but you'll be given ample time off to take care of personal affairs and to rest up for your next sea cruise.

The Navy is not as regimented in terms of military "spit 'n polish" as is the Marine Corps. But things aren't as relaxed as they are in the Air Force. Haircuts are relatively short, and beards are now out, even though a few years ago they were allowed.

Sailors pay a lot of attention to rank. Officers have a lot of prestige, noncommissioned officers are looked up to and respected, and failure to comply with military regulations is frowned upon. If you err, you won't have to walk the plank, but you won't merely have your wrist slapped either. Transgressions are dealt with fairly and firmly.

THE ARMY

"The green machine," it's called . . . the U.S. Army, largest of our five military services. There are over 775,000 soldiers in the Army. They're located around the world, though they're mostly found in Alaska, Hawaii, Panama, Germany, Korea, and, of course, in the continental United States.

The Army is at the very core of our nation's defense structure. Though the Navy may offer the adventure of travel, the Air Force boasts the glamour of air and space, and the Marines has the aura of the tough fighter, the Army has a special significance and image all its own. The foot soldier and the tank crew led by capable leaders like MacArthur, Eisenhower, Patton, and Bradley; all contribute to the overall image of the U.S. Army.

Role and Mission

The Army's primary mission is to defend and attack on land when war breaks out—the toughest and most dangerous job of all. The soldier is in the front line, firing and being fired on. He is vulnerable and he must be brave and courageous.

Army troops are stationed on the borders of conflict. In Europe, four divisions—300,000 soldiers—are in Germany, awaiting a possible attack by communist forces of the Warsaw Pact nations, the Soviet Union, East Germany, and others. In Korea, another Army division sits, ready for battle in case the North Koreans decide to give war another try.

Back home in the United States the Army has 11 divisions, including one in Alaska. These forces represent the defense of our homes and cities. Without them, the path to victory would be fairly swift for a would-be conqueror. Most of these forces are infantry—the heart of the Army, affectionately known as "legs," "groundpounders," "GI Joes," and "dusteaters."

At Fort Bragg, North Carolina, the Army has the 18th Airborne—the paratroopers. On short notice, these hard, ready troops can be airlifted by Air Force C-130's and other planes directly into a battle theater anywhere in the world. Also at Fort Bragg is the headquarters of the Special Forces—the Green Berets. The Green Berets are highly trained warriors qualified and ready to serve in a number of areas—communications, intelligence, weapons, and medicine. They can operate in any type of environment; snow, jungle, or desert, and they are trained in many languages.

The Army's most elite units are those of the Rangers. These men are the "soldiers' soldiers." They are trained to go anywhere, to parachute, to descend from helicopters, and to fight against amazing odds in all kinds of terrain and weather. They specialize in reconnaissance missions behind enemy lines. Obviously, the Rangers only want dedicated people willing to endure self-discipline and capable of a grim determination as well as teamwork.

Whatever the specific combat task of an Army unit, whether infantry armor, artillery, Ranger or other, the Army is our prime combat "force." The fact is that the Air Force can bombard a place to smithereens, the Navy can sail its ships close to shore, and the Marines can provide a rapid shock force, but the Army is ready for the long haul on land. Someone has to go in and take territory, or defend it. In the U.S. military, that someone is the soldier.

Composition

The Army is composed of personnel who perform duties in a wide-ranging variety of occupations. Unlike the Air Force and Navy, however, many of the occupational skills are not transferable to civilian life. This limits the attraction of Army service to many youth, especially those who join the military to acquire job training and experience.

The commonly held view that nearly everyone in the Army is a ground soldier is false. Only about one-fourth of Army personnel are assigned direct combat jobs. The others work in fields such as electronics, computers, supply, administration, engineering, medical services, and military police. Like the other services, the

Army operates a huge training system to teach its personnel needed skills. Many of the Army's training programs have been praised by civilian accrediting agencies and civilian employers as rivaling or exceeding those found in civilian vocational schools and colleges.

Army troops serve all over the world. Nearly one-third are overseas at any given time, so the opportunity to travel is one advantage for persons who enlist in this branch.

Life-style

The life-style of the average American soldier has dramatically improved over the last decade or so. Many irritants of service life have been removed. Reveille (wake-up) has been eliminated, new facilities for recreation have been built, and education programs have been expanded and pay improved.

Single persons live in dormitories with two to four persons to a room. Much like college dorms, much of the housing for single Army personnel has areas for lounging, refrigerators, recreation rooms with pool tables, video games and ping pong equipment, and assorted vending machines. Although the dormitories are expected to be maintained in a clean and orderly condition, there are no "white glove" inspections. Live decently, make your bed, empty the trash can regularly, keep the floor swept and clean, and you should not have a problem with your superiors.

Army discipline and military regimen is harsher than that in the Air Force, but it is certainly not enforced to the degree you would find in the Marine Corps. Haircuts for men are short, but not ridiculously so. Women may wear their hair in almost any style, but it may not extend past their collar.

The Army stresses physical fitness and many units engage in fitness programs as a group. This is especially true of combat-ready units like the 18th Airborne Corps, the Rangers, and many others. Things are a little more relaxed for support units, but soldiers are always expected to stay in shape, and time off from duties is usually given for a person to participate in organized sports. Also, all Army supervisors are generous in granting time off for individual exercise programs.

As a combat force, the Army pays heed to the traditional rules of rank and status. Officers are definitely in charge, but senior noncommissioned officers have a lot of discretion in carrying out orders and supervising the day-to-day operation of units.

THE COAST GUARD

Is the Coast Guard a military service? Many don't think so. The fact that this service falls under the jurisdiction of the Department of Transportation in peacetime leads many to the conclusion that the Coast Guard is not a branch of the military. This is definitely a wrong conclusion, however, as the Coast Guard has all the organizational elements of a military service and, indeed, comes under the direction of the Navy in wartime.

In World War II, the Coast Guard actively fought and sunk German U-boats and suffered many war casualties.

During the Vietnam War, the Coast Guard operated 22 cutters (small, fast-moving ships) in waterways in Vietnam and also in neighboring Thailand. These Coast Guard vessels were assigned the task of stopping the infiltration of enemy junks (small makeshift boats), which were capable of moving through narrow waterways to resupply communist forces.

The Coast Guard is proud of its contributions to our nation's defense, as well as the unique nature of other tasks it is assigned.

Role and Mission

The Coast Guard is the only branch of service with a broad peacetime mission. This service is responsible for safeguarding our nation's coasts. In meeting the responsibility, the Coast Guard maintains hundreds of navigation and rescue stations, collects oceanographic data for environmental research, enforces pollution regulations in waterways, arrests smugglers, drug runners and foreign poachers, and assists in boat safety programs.

The rescue mission of the Coast Guard is vital, and thousands of persons owe their lives to the skills and bravery of well-trained Coast Guard crews. In a typical year, the Coast Guard receives about 70,000 calls for assistance on the water, saves 4,200 persons from death, aids another 140,000, and saves over $280 million of endangered property.

Throughout America's inland waters and along her coastal borders, the Coast Guard maintains rescue stations manned around the clock, ready to launch small boats within minutes of a distress call. The Coast Guard's 26 air stations are also on 24-hour call, ready to lend search assistance or to perform rescues when vessel rescue isn't possible. The vital communications necessary to coordinate the work of these units is handled through the Coast Guard's net of district Rescue Coordination Centers (RCC), which are backed up by Pacific and Atlantic commands and, ultimately, by a national communications nerve center located at Coast Guard Headquarters. The result is a national search and rescue effort, ready to respond to any threat to life and property on the water, from an overturned rowboat to a major maritime disaster.

The Coast Guard also participates in the International Ice Patrol, begun in 1913 as a result of the Titanic disaster. Each year, the Coast Guard, assisted by other member nations that use these sea lanes, patrols a 45,000-square-mile area, including the North Atlantic sea lanes and the Grand Banks fishing grounds. In an average year, 200 to 400 icebergs are tracked. Occasionally, the figure jumps to as many as 1,000.

Composition

The Coast Guard fleet has over 300 large cutters and ships, hundreds of smaller craft, a large number of helicopters, and many small aircraft. Operating this flotilla of water-going vessels and aircraft are about 37,000 persons. This makes the Coast Guard by far the smallest of the nation's five military branches.

Most of the occupations held by Coast Guard members are also found in the Navy. This is understandable as the Coast Guard, like the Navy, is an ocean- and water-based service. Coast Guard personnel perform duties as electricians, boatswains, boiler technicians, hull repairmen, carpenters, mechanical engineers, and in many other highly technical skilled trades.

Life-style

Coast Guard personnel probably spend more time on the water, as a general rule, than do Navy personnel. They are stationed at small sites and installations, so the supporting base structures are quite limited. The Coast Guard is thus not able to maintain the elaborate system of hospitals, commissaries, and exchange stores the other services operate. Their life-style suffers as a result.

However, the Coast Guard operates the majority of its units adjacent to or in large cities and populated coastal areas. This means that its personnel have access to the off-duty pursuits and activities of these communities. This compensates somewhat for the lack of facilities at the Coast Guard installations.

Coast Guard personnel are often trained in several specialties, and each person performs a wide range of duties. This is necessary because its cutters and other craft are small and cannot afford the luxury of having specialists assigned in many fields. So, Coast Guard personnel have the opportunity to become a "jack of all trades."

Life aboard a Coast Guard cutter is similar to Navy life except amenities are more limited. A family-type atmosphere and a mutual feeling of teamwork and cooperation makes sea duty a little more bearable.

If you join the Coast Guard, expect to be forced to continually explain to your civilian friends just what it is the Coast Guard does. Most civilians find it hard to comprehend the diverse mission of the Coast Guard and are prone to equate it with other federal agencies such as the Border Patrol, the Immigration Service, and the Drug Enforcement Agency. You will then have the task of describing the many important duties of your service to an interested public, assuring them that, yes, the Coast Guard is a branch of the military.

SUMMARY

Well, which service is right for you? As I said at the beginning of this chapter, each service has its advantages and disadvantages and each plays a vital and significant role in our nation's security.

If you haven't yet made up your mind, perhaps it is because you want to first find out more about each of the services. For instance, what education and training opportunities do they offer, where do they assign their people, and what opportunities exist for career advancement? And even more important, what occupational and career specialties do they offer? In the following chapter, we'll tackle this last question and help you nail down the answer to which service is right for you.

5. Occupational Fields

$200,000! That's how much it costs the Air Force to train one pilot! Perhaps that's why the civilian airlines hire the majority of their pilots directly from the services. However, it's not just pilots that cost a fortune to train. It is estimated that the Navy spends $50,000 to train one electronics technician, the Army shells out an equal amount to qualify an avionics mechanic, and the Marine Corps is out over $60,000 on each air traffic controller trained.

Young American men and women recognize the fantastic investment the services make in training people to perform the complicated technical duties of a modern military force. According to a recent study, the chance to learn a valuable skill is the single most important reason why persons 16 to 21 years old enter the armed forces.

Most military occupations are directly transferable to the civilian work world. And, in fact, if it were not for the training and job skills acquired in military service, several million skilled civilian workers—trained by the military, and now veterans—would either be unemployed or working in an unskilled job that pays much less. Civilian employers well recognize the value of service occupations and they place a lot of stock in the job experience and skills of ex-service people.

This chapter provides you with a complete listing of all the occupations or career fields found in the armed forces. It was compiled by the services themselves and first published in the Department of Defense publication, *Profile*. It is an excellent source and not only lists each career field but also the typical duties and responsibilities of a person assigned to the field.

If you're thinking of doing your time in uniform and then rejoining civilian life, examine this list. You'll find that almost every skill found in the civilian labor force is duplicated in the military. This is what makes military job experience so rewarding. Regardless of the field you're most interested in, the military will train you and give you several years of valuable on-the-job experience.

The listing of military occupations includes the qualifications you will need to be assigned duty in the career field. Don't let this throw you. The services write the list of qualifications for a field in such a way that, upon reading them, you may immediately and mistakenly come to the conclusion that you don't meet them. For instance, take the first Air Force career field shown—Accounting, Finance, and Auditing. Qualifications for this field are described as follows:

> Dexterity in the operation of business machines. Typing, mathematics, statistics, and accounting desirable. High administrative aptitude mandatory.

Note that "typing, mathematics, statistics, and accounting" are "desirable." Let me repeat that word: "desirable." They are not "mandatory." If you want this career field, there are only two "mandatory" qualifications, "dexterity in the operation of business machines" and a "high administrative aptitude." If your fingers and wrists are normal, they are dexterous, and if you do reasonably well on the

administrative portion of the ASVAB service exam, you meet the "high administrative aptitude" qualification.

So, watch for words like *desirable* and *helpful*. These are not disqualifying terms and you may still qualify if you meet other requirements. These abilities may help you to get assigned to a career field, but lacking them won't necessarily keep you from getting it.

Also, pay attention to the column Examples of Civilian Jobs. This tells you what civilian jobs are comparable to the military career field. For example, the Armor career field in the Army is comparable to such civilian jobs as heavy equipment operator or foreman supervisor. So, as you can see, even occupations and fields which in the military are combat-related may surprisingly have some transferability and applicability to civilian jobs.

OCCUPATIONAL FIELDS FOR ENLISTED PERSONNEL*

Air Force

Career Fields	Duties & Responsibilities	Qualifications	Examples of Civilian Jobs
Accounting, Finance and Auditing	Prepares documents required to account for and disburses funds, including budgeting, allocation, disbursing, auditing and the preparation of cost analysis records.	Dexterity in the operation of business machines. Typing, mathematics, statistics and accounting desirable. High administrative aptitude mandatory.	Cost and public accountant, auditor, bookkeeper, budget clerk and paymaster.
Administrative	Prepares correspondence, statistical summaries, and arranges priority and distribution systems, maintains files, prepares and consolidates reports and arranges for graphic presentations.	English, typing, accounting, mathematics and shorthand courses desirable.	Clerk typist, file clerk, secretary, stenographer, receptionist.
Aircraft Maintenance	Performs the mechanical functions of maintenance, repair, and modification of helicopters, turbo-prop, reciprocating engine and jet aircraft.	Considerable mechanical or electrical aptitude and manual dexterity. Shop mathematics and physics desirable.	Aircraft mechanic, plane inspector.
Aircraft Systems Maintenance	Performs maintenance of aircraft accessory and propulsion systems, fabricates metal and fabric materials used in aircraft structural repair, and inspection and preservation of aircraft materials.	Considerable electrical and mechanical aptitude; shop mathematics and shopwork is desirable.	Aircraft mechanic, aircraft electrician, sheet metal worker, welder, machinist.
Aircrew Protection	Performs instruction on the use of survival techniques and protective equipment.	Good physical condition required; knowledge of pioneering and woodsman activities helpful.	No civilian job covers the scope of the jobs in this career field, but a related job is that of a hunting or fishing guide.
Audio-Visual	Operates aerial and ground cameras, motion picture and other photographic equipment; processes photographs and film, edits motion pictures, performs photographic instrumentation functions, and operates airborne, field and precision processing laboratories.	Considerable dexterity on small precision equipment, excellent eyesight. Mathematics, physics and chemistry desirable.	Cameraman, darkroom man, film editor, aerial commercial photographer, photograph finisher, sound mixer and motion picture operator.

*Reprinted with permission of *Profile* magazine.

47

Career Fields	Duties & Responsibilities	Qualifications	Examples of Civilian Jobs
Avionics Systems	Installs, maintains and repairs airborne bomb navigation, fire control, weapon control, automatic flight control systems, radio and navigation equipment, electronic warfare equipment and maintains associated test equipment.	Electronic aptitude, manual dexterity and normal vision. Mathematics, physics desirable.	Radar, television and precision instrument maintenance.
Band	Plays musical instruments in concert bands and orchestras, repairs and maintains instruments, sings in glee clubs, performs as drum major, arranges music and maintains music libraries.	Knowledge of rudiments of music, elementary theory of music and orchestration desirable.	Orchestrator, music librarian, music teacher, instrumental musician.
Communication-Electronics Systems	Installs, modifies, maintains repairs and overhauls airborne and ground television equipment, high speed general and special purpose data processing equipment, automatic communications and cryptographic machines systems, teletypewriter, teleautographic equipment, telecommunications systems control and associated electronic test equipment.	Basic knowledge of electronic theory. Mathematics and physics desirable. Normal color vision mandatory.	Communications, electronics technician, radio and television repairer, meteorological and teletype equipment repairer.
Communications Operations	Operates radio and wire communications systems, automatic digital switching equipment, cryptographic devices, airborne and ground electronic countermeasures equipment, all kinds of communication equipment, and the management of radio frequencies.	Knowledge of telecommunications functions and operations of electronic communications equipment. Typing and clear speaking voice desirable in many specialties.	Central office operator (telephone and telegraph), cryptographer, radio operator, telephone supervisor and photo-radio operator.
Computer Systems	Collects, processes, records, prepares and submits data for various automated systems, analyzes design, programs and operates computer systems.	Business arithmetic, algebra, geometry desirable.	Card-tape converter or computer operator, data typist, data processing control clerk, high-speed printer operator, programmer.
Contracting/ Manufacturing	Acquires material and services for support of military installations; involves advertising or negotiating bids and awarding contracts.	General aptitude for business and clerical work; business arithmetic and bookkeeping courses desirable.	Purchasing agent, contract negotiator, contract specialist, procurement, field, general clerk.
Control Systems Operations	Operates control towers, directs aircraft landings with radar landing control equipment; operates ground radar equipment, aircraft control centers, airborne radar equipment, space tracking and missile warning systems.	Equipment dexterity, clear voice and speech ability and excellent vision. English desirable.	Aircraft log clerk, airport control operator and air traffic controller.
Dental	Operates dental facilities and provides paraprofessional dental care; preventive dental services, treatment of oral tissues and fabrication of prosthetic devices.	Knowledge of oral and dental anatomy; physiology, biology and chemistry desirable.	Dental hygienist, dental assistant.
Education and Training	Conducts formal classes of instruction, uses training aids, develops material for various courses of instruction and teaches classes in general academic subjects and military matters.	English composition and speech desirable.	Vocational training instructor, counselor, educational consultant.

Career Fields	Duties & Responsibilities	Qualifications	Examples of Civilian Jobs
Enlisted Aircrew	Primary duties require frequent and regular flights. Inflight Refueling Operator performs duties associated with inflight refueling of aircraft; Defense Aerial Gunner is a B-52 integrated crewmember with responsibility for defense of the aircraft; Aircraft Loadmaster supervises loading of cargo and passengers and operates aircraft equipment; Pararescue/Recovery personnel perform aircrew protection skills; and Flight Engineers ensure mechanical condition of the aircraft and monitor inflight aircraft systems.	High electrical and mechanical aptitude, manual dexterity, normal vision and good physical condition. Mathematics, physics and shopwork desirable.	Aircraft mechanic, electrician, engineman, carburetor man, hydraulic tester, oxygen systems tester, cargo handler, dispatcher and shipping clerk depending upon the area in which training and experience is received. No civilian job covers some aspects of this field.
Fire Protection	Operates firefighting equipment, prevents and extinguishes aircraft and structural fires; rescues and renders first aid; maintains firefighting and fire prevention equipment.	Good physical condition; no allergies to oil and fire extinguishing solutions; general science and chemistry desirable.	Fire chief, fire extinguisher serviceman, fireman, fire marshal and fire department equipmentman.
Fuels	Receives, stores, dispenses, tests and inspects propellants, petroleum fuels and products.	Chemistry and arithmetic.	Petroleum industry foreman and bulk plant manager.
Intelligence	Collects, produces and disseminates data of strategic, tactical or technical value from an intelligence viewpoint. Maintains information security.	Knowledge of techniques of evaluation, analysis, interpretation and reporting. Foreign languages, English composition, photography and mathematics desirable.	Cryptanalyst, draftsman, interpreter, investigator, statistician, radio operator and translator.
Intricate Equipment Maintenance	Overhauls and modifies photographic equipment; works with fine precision tools, testing devices and schematic drawings.	Considerable mechanical ability and manual dexterity; algebra and physics desirable.	Camera repairer, statistical machine and medical equipment serviceman.
Legal	Takes and transcribes verbal recordings of legal proceedings; uses stenomask; performs office administrative tasks; processes claims.	Knowledge of stenomask, typewriter, legal terminology, military legal procedures, preparation and processing of claims; English grammar and composition; ability to take dictation by stenomask at 175 words per minute, type 50 words per minute and speak clearly and distinctly.	Law librarian, court clerk and shorthand reporter.
Management Analysis	Collects, processes, records, controls, analyzes, and interprets special and recurring reports, statistical data and other information.	Knowledge of business statistics, mathematics, accounting and English desirable. Completion of high school or GED equivalent mandatory.	Statistical, accounting and budget clerk.
Manpower Management	Performs management studies and evaluates work requirements to determine manpower required to accomplish Air Force jobs. Conducts management consultant studies.	Completion of high school or GED equivalency with courses in mathematics, including algebra and high general aptitude mandatory.	Industrial engineering technician, management and job analyst.
Marine	Performs duties in the operation and maintenance of boats, deck equipment, gasoline or diesel engines, and prepares boats and related equipment for storage, uses utility craft, inspects and repairs mechanical, electrical, and sanitary marine equipment and maintains boat structure.	Mechanical aptitude, normal color vision and high vision; normal depth perception, hearing, and gait and balance; no record of acrophobia and physical ability to perform climbing duties; no record of hydrophobia.	Ordinary seaman, motorboat operator, ship electrician, marine engine machinist, motorboat mechanic, marine oiler.

Career Fields	Duties & Responsibilities	Qualifications	Examples of Civilian Jobs
Mechanical/ Electrical	Performs installation, operation, maintenance and repairs of air and missile base direct support systems and equipment and missile weapon systems support facilities.	Physics, mathematics, blueprint reading and electricity.	Elevator repairer, electrician, lineman, powerhouse repairer, diesel mechanic, pipefitter, steamfitter and heating and ventilating worker.
Medical	Operates medical facilities, works with professional medical staff as they provide care and treatment. May specialize in such medical services as nuclear medicine, cardiopulmonary techniques, physical and occupational therapy, orthotic appliances, medical laboratory, veterinary and medical administrative services.	Knowledge of first aid, ability to help professional medical personnel; anatomy, biology, zoology. High school algebra and chemistry desirable in most specialties and are mandatory requirements for some.	X-ray, and medical record technician, medical laboratory and pharmacist assistant. Respiratory therapy technician and surgical technologist.
Missile Electronics Maintenance	Assembles, installs, maintains, checks out, repairs, and modifies missile and drone guidance, control, analyst, launches, test equipment, and instrumentation systems and related missile and drone subsystems.	Knowledge of basic electronic theory and circuits, hydraulics. Normal color vision mandatory.	Missile facilities repairer, electronics engineer, electronics inspector, electronics mechanic, and aircraft mechanical-electrical system repairer.
Missile Maintenance	Performs missile engine installation, maintenance and repair; maintenance, repair and modification of missile airframes, subsystems and associated aerospace ground equipment.	Mechanical aptitude and manual dexterity. Mathematics and physics desirable. Normal color vision mandatory.	Mechanical inspector, mechanical engineer, aircraft mechanic, and pneumatic tester and mechanic.
Motor Vehicle Maintenance	Overhauls and maintains powered ground vehicles and mechanical equipment for transporting personnel, supplies and such work as airfield construction.	Machine shop, mathematics and training in the use of tools and blueprints helpful.	Automobile accessories installer, automobile repairer, bus mechanic, carburetor man, automotive electrician and truck mechanic.
Munitions and Weapons Maintenance	Maintains and repairs aircraft armament, assembles, maintains, loads, unloads, stores munitions and nuclear weapons, disposes of bombs, missiles and rockets and operates detection instruments.	Mechanical or electrical aptitude, manual dexterity, normal color vision and depth perception; mathematics and mechanics desirable.	Aircraft armament mechanic, armorer, ammunition inspector, munitions handler.
Personnel	Interviews, classifies, selects career jobs for airmen on the basis of qualifications and requirements of the Air Force; administers aptitude, performance tests; administers personnel quality control programs; performs counseling, educational and administrative functions in support of Social Action programs.	English composition, speech and social sciences. Operation of simple data processing equipment and typing ability desirable.	Employment, or personnel clerk, special services supervisor, personnel service manager, personnel supervisor, counselor.
Photomapping	Procures, compiles, computes and uses topographic, photogrammetric, and cartographic data in preparing aeronautical charts, topographic maps and target folders.	Ability to use precision instruments required in measuring and drafting; algebra, geometry, trigonometry and physics necessary.	Map draftsman, topographical draftsman, mapmaker, cartographer, compass man and advertising layout man.
Printing	Operates and maintains reproduction equipment used in the graphic arts, performs hand and machine composition and binding operations.	Mechanical ability and dexterity; courses in chemistry and shop mechanics desirable.	Lithographic press, fold machine, offset and webpress, perforating machine or duplicating machine operator; bookbinder; photolithographer; photoengraver.

Career Fields	Duties & Responsibilities	Qualifications	Examples of Civilian Jobs
Public Affairs	Interviews people; reports news; composes, proofreads, writes and edits news copy; provides public affairs advice.	High general aptitude and completion of high school or GED equivalency mandatory. English grammar and composition, speech, journalism, drama, radio/ television, history, or political science desirable.	Reporter, copy reader, historian, public relations representative, editorial assistant, broadcast or program director, announcer.
Safety	Conducts safety programs, surveys areas and activities to eliminate hazards, analyzes accident causes and trends.	Knowledge of industrial hygiene, safety education, safety psychology, and blueprint interpretation; typing, English and public speaking desirable.	Safety inspector and instructor.
Sanitation	Operates and maintains water and waste processing plants' systems and equipment and performs pest and rodent control functions.	Physics, biology, chemistry and blueprint reading valuable.	Purification plant operator, sanitary inspector, exterminator and entomologist.
Security Police	Provide security for classified information and material, enforce law and order, control traffic, and protect lives and property, organize as local ground defense forces.	Good physical condition, vision and hearing; civics and social sciences desirable.	Guard, police inspector, police officer, watchman and superintendent of police.
Special Investigations/ Counterintelligence	Investigates violations of the Uniform Code of Military Justice and applicable Federal statutes, investigates conditions pertaining to sabotage, espionage, treason, sedition, and security.	Knowledge of law enforcement and security regulations, good physical condition, hearing and vision; civics, social sciences, accounting and foreign language desirable.	Detective, chief of detectives, detective sergeant and investigator.
Morale, Welfare and Recreation	Conducts physical conditioning, coaches sports program, administers recreation, entertainment, sports and club activities.	Good muscular coordination; English business arithmetic and physical education desirable.	Athletic or playground director, physical instructor and manager of a recreational establishment.
Structural/ Pavements	Constructs and maintains structural facilities and pavement areas; maintains pavements, railroads and soil bases; performs erosion control; operates heavy equipment; and performs site development, general maintenance, cost and real property accounting, work control functions and metal fabricating.	Blueprint reading, mechanical drawing, mathematics, physics, and chemistry.	Plumber, bricklayer, carpenter, stonemason, painter, construction worker, welder and sheet metal worker.
Supply	Designs, develops, analyzes and operates supply systems including supply data systems; responsible for computation, operation and management of material facilities; equipment review and validation; records maintenance, inventory and distribution control; budget computation and financial plans.	Accounting and business administration.	Junior accountant, machine records section supervisor, receiving, shipping and stock clerk.
Supply Services	Supervises and operates sales stores, laundry/dry cleaning facilities, commissaries and meat processing. Cooks and bakes.	Chemistry, management, marketing, manual dexterity and business mathematics.	Department manager, retail general merchandise manager, meat cutter, butcher, chef and pastry cook.
Training Devices	Installs, operates, repairs, and modifies instrument, navigation, bombing gunnery trainers and flight simulators; works with small tools and precision test equipment.	Knowledge of electricity, mathematics, blueprint reading and physics desirable.	Link trainer instructor, radio mechanic.
Transportation	Ensures service, efficiency and economy of transportation of supplies and personnel by aircraft, train, motor vehicle and ship.	Driver training, operation of office machines and business arithmetic.	Cargo handler, motor vehicle dispatcher, shipping or traffic rate clerk, trailer truck driver and ticket agent.

Career Fields	Duties & Responsibilities	Qualifications	Examples of Civilian Jobs
Wire Communications Systems Maintenance	Installs and maintains wire communications equipment and systems. Installs, repairs and maintains telephone and telegraph land line systems, telephone equipment, antenna support systems, key systems, telephone switching equipment, missile communications control systems and electronic switching equipment.	Mechanical aptitude and manual dexterity; physics and mathematics desirable. Normal color perception mandatory. Physical ability to climb required in some specialties.	Cable splicer, central office repairer, line installer and inspector, telephone inspector, teletype and central office manual equipment repairer.
Weather	Collects, records and analyzes meteorological data; makes visual and instrument weather observations. Forecast immediate and long-range weather conditions.	Visual acuity correctable to 20/20; physics, mathematics and geography desirable.	Meteorologist, weather forecaster and weather observer.

Army

Career Fields	Duties & Responsibilities	Qualifications	Examples of Civilian Jobs
Armor (C)	Performs combat tasks using tanks and armored reconnaissance vehicles.	Team sports, mechanical maintenance, orienteering	Heavy equipment operator, foreman, supervisor
Combat Engineering	Constructs and maintains roads and bridges, operates powered bridges, constructs minefields and installs booby traps, demolitions with high explosives, erects temporary shelters and sets up camouflage.	Automotive mechanics, carpentry, woodworking, mechanical drawing and drafting courses.	Blaster, construction equipment operator, construction supervisor, bridge repairer and lumber worker.
Infantry (C)	Performs combat tasks using rifles, mortars, tank destroying missiles, personnel carriers, vehicle-mounted guns and fire control equipment.	Team sports, orienteering, hunting and other outdoor sports.	Foreman, supervisor, gunsmith, security officer, firearms handler.
Administration	Performs general administrative duties such as typing, stenography and postal functions and specialized administrative duties such as personnel, legal, club management, equal opportunity and chapel activities.	Basic clerical and communication abilities, typing, bookkeeping, stenography or office management skills desirable.	Clerk typist, secretary, employment interviewer, postal clerk, recreation specialist, office manager, personnel clerk, bookkeeper, cashier, payroll clerk, court clerk, and restaurant, cafeteria or liquor establishment manager.
Air Defense Artillery (*)	Emplaces, assembles, tests, maintains and fires air defense weapons systems; operates fire control equipment, radars, computers, automatic data transmission and associated power supply equipment.	Basic mechanical, electrical, electronic and mathematical abilities; emotional stability and high degree of reasoning ability.	Map and topographical drafter, cartographer.
Air Defense Missile Maintenance	Inspects, tests, maintains and repairs guided missile fire control equipment and related radar installations which guide missiles their target.	Mathematics, physics, electricity and electronics.	Radio installation and repair inspector, electronic equipment technician, radio and TV repairer.
Ammunition	Handles, stores, reconditions and salvages ammunition, explosives, and components; locates, removes and destroys or salvages unexploded bombs and missiles.	Mechanical aptitude, attentiveness, good close vision, normal color discrimination, manual dexterity and hand-eye coordination.	Toxic chemical handler, ammunition inspector and acid plant operator.

(C) indicates combat-related groups closed to women.

(*) indicates groups generally open to all applicants, but may include specific combat-related positions available only to men.

Career Fields	Duties & Responsibilities	Qualifications	Examples of Civilian Jobs
Automatic Data Processing	Operates a variety of electric accounting and automatic data processing equipment to produce personnel, supply, fiscal, medical, intelligence and other reports.	Reasoning and verbal ability, clerical aptitude, finger and manual dexterity and hand-eye coordination. Knowledge of typing and office machines.	Coding clerk, key punch, computer and sorting machine operator, machine records unit supervisor.
Aviation Communications-Electronic Systems Maintenance	Repairs and maintains navigation, flight control, ground control approach radar, aerial surveillance and associated communications equipment.	Electrical/electronic theory and repair.	Electronics technician, radar repairer, electrical instrument mechanic/repairer.
Aviation Maintenance	Performs general maintenance on fixed-wing and rotary-wing aircraft. Operates and maintains aircraft weapon systems and serves as flying crew chief.	Aircraft and automotive mechanics, blueprint reading, electricity, sheet metal working, mathematics and physics.	Aircraft engine mechanic, airframe repairer, airplane electrician and aircraft fuel systems mechanic.
Ballistic/Land Combat Missile and Light Air Defense Weapons System Maintenance	Inspects, tests, maintains and repairs tactical missile systems and related test equipment and trainers.	Mathematics, physics, electricity, electronics (radio and TV) and blueprint reading.	Electronic equipment technician, radio electrician and mechanic, TV repair and service technician.
Band	Plays brass, woodwind or percussion instrument in marching, concert, dance, stage and show bands, combos or instrumental ensembles. Sings in vocal group, writes and arranges music.	Instrumental audition on brass, woodwind or percussion instrument.	Bandsperson, bandmaster, musician, accompanist, arranger, music director, orchestrator, music teacher, orchestra leader and vocalist.
Chemical	Provides decontamination service after chemical, biological or radiological attacks, produces smoke for battlefield concealment, repairs chemical equipment and assists in overall planning of chemical, biological, or radiological activities.	Biology, chemistry and electricity.	Laboratory assistant (biological, chemical or radiological), pumper and repairer (chemical) and exterminator.
Communications-Electronics Maintenance	Installs, maintains radar and radio receiving, transmitting, carrier and terminal equipment.	Electricity, mathematics, electronics and blueprint reading.	Radio control room technician, radio mechanic, transmitter, radio and TV repairer.
Communications-Electronics Operations	Installs, maintains field telephone switchboards and field radio communications equipment.	Mathematics, physics and shop courses in electricity.	Communications engineer assistant, plant wireman and radio electrician or operator.
Electronic Warfare Cryptologic Operations	Collects and analyzes electromagnetic emissions; ensures communications security; performs electronic warfare duties in fixed or mobile operations.	Verbal and reasoning ability and perceptual speed; aural and visual acuity.	Radio and telegraph operator, navigator, intelligence research analyst, statistician, signal collection technician.
Electronic Warfare Intercept Systems Maintenance	Installs, operates and maintains intercept, electronic measuring and testing equipment.	Physics, mathematics, electricity, electronics (radio and TV) and blueprint reading.	Electrical instrument, meteorological instrument repairer and electronic equipment inspector.
Finance And Accounting	Maintains pay records of military personnel; prepares vouchers for payment; prepares reports, disburses funds; accounts for funds, to include budgeting, allocation, and auditing; compiles and analyzes statistical data and prepares cost analysis records.	Dexterity in the operation of business machines. Typing, mathematics, statistics and basic principles of accounting desirable. High administrative aptitude mandatory.	Paymaster, cashier, statistical or audit clerk, accountant, budget clerk and bookkeeper

Career Fields	Duties & Responsibilities	Qualifications	Examples of Civilian Jobs
Public Affairs and Audio-Visual	Prepares newspaper, radio and television communications; maintains radio and television equipment; performs still and motion picture photography, audio-visual equipment repair; produces graphic illustrations.	Clerical aptitude, emotional control, verbal ability, auditory acuity, color vision, manual dexterity.	Electronics mechanic, television repairer, reporter, editor, script writer, announcer, sign painter, illustrator.
Recruitment and Retention	Contacts prospective enlistees and reenlistees; counsels about job and career opportunities; performs administrative duties associated with personnel enlistment/reenlistment.	Reasoning ability, clarity of speech and ability to work independent of direct supervision. Personnel in recruiting must be E-5 or above and have completed two years service. Those in reenlistment must be E-6 or above and have completed six years service.	Personnel and training administration occupations, occupational analyst, personnel administration.
Supply and Service	Receives, stores and issues individual, organizational and expendable supplies, equipment and spare parts; establishes, posts and maintains stock records; repairs and alters textile, canvas and leather supplies, rigs parachutes, decontaminates materials. Performs grave registration functions.	Arithmetic ability and perceptual speed in scanning and checking supply documents. Verbal ability; courses in bookkeeping, typing and office machine operation.	Inventory clerk, stock control clerk or supervisor, shipping or parts clerk, warehouse manager, parachute rigger and funeral attendant.
Topographic Engineering	Performs land survey; produces construction drawings and plans, maps, charts, diagrams and illustrated material; constructs scale models of terrain and structures. Operates offset duplicators, presses and bindery equipment. Repairs survey instruments and reproduction equipment.	Mechanical drawing and drafting, blueprint reading, commercial art, fine arts, geography and mathematics.	Drafting (structural, mechanical and topographical), cartographic and art layout, model maker, commercial artist and physical geographer.
Transportation	Operates and performs preventive maintenance on passenger, light, medium and heavy cargo vehicles; operates and maintains marine lighterage and harbor craft; performs as air traffic controller.	Mechanical aptitude, manual dexterity, hand-eye coordination, FAA certification for air traffic control, license for vehicle operation.	Truck driver, FAA air traffic controller.

Marine Corps

Career Fields	Duties & Responsibilities	Qualifications	Examples of Civilian Jobs
Field Artillery (C)	Maintains rocket and missile batteries, heavy mortars and self-propelled 175mm guns, 8-inch and 105mm howitzers.	Arithmetical reasoning, mechanical aptitude, good vision and stamina; mechanics, electricity, meteorology and mathematics.	Surveyor, geodetic computer, meteorologist, radio operator, recording engineer and ordnance inspector.
Infantry (C)	Performs as rifleman, machine gunner, or grenadier; infantry unit leader, supervises training and operations of infantry units.	Verbal and arithmetic reasoning, good vision and stamina; general mathematics, mechanical drafting, geography and mechanical drawing.	Firearms assembler, gunsmith, policeman, immigration inspector and plant security policeman.
Tank and Amphibian Tractor (C)	Performs as driver, gunner and loaders in tanks, armored amphibious tractors.	Mechanical ability and stamina; auto mechanics, machine shop electricity and mechanical drawing.	Automotive mechanic, bulldozer operator or repairman, caterpillar repairman, armament machinist-mechanic and gunsmith assistant.

Career Fields	Duties & Responsibilities	Qualifications	Examples of Civilian Jobs
Field Artillery (*)	Operates, maintains and directs fire of field artillery guns, howitzers, missiles, rockets and related weapons. Operates and maintains supporting equipment such as target acquisition radars, sound and flash ranging, meteorological and survey equipment.	Emotional stability, arithmetic and reasoning abilities.	Map and topographical drafter, cartographer, surveyor, weather chart preparer.
Food Service	Plans regular and special diet menus. Cooks and bakes food in dining facilities and during field exercises. Serves as aide and cook on personal staff of general officer.	Home economics, work in a restaurant, bake shop or meat market.	Cook, chef, caterer, baker, butcher, kitchen supervisor and cafeteria manager.
General Engineering	Provides utilities and engineering services such as electric power production, building and roadway construction and maintenance, salvage activities, airstrip construction, water purification, storage tank and pipeline construction, firefighting and crash rescue operations.	Mechanical aptitude, emotional stability and ability to visualize spatial relationships. Carpentry, woodworking or mechanical drawing.	Carpenter, construction equipment operator, electrician, firefighter, driver, plumber, welder, bricklayer.
Law Enforcement	Enforces military regulations; protects facilities, roads and designated sensitive areas and personnel; controls traffic movement; guards military prisoners and enemy prisoners of war; investigates traffic accidents and crimes involving military personnel.	Sociology and demonstrated prowess and leadership in athletics and other group work helpful.	Police officer, plant guard, detective, investigator, crime detection laboratory assistant and ballistics expert.
Mechanical Maintenance	Services and repairs land and amphibious wheel and tracked vehicles ranging from cars and light trucks to heavy tanks and self-propelled weapons; installs and repairs refrigeration, bakery and laundry equipment.	Automotive mechanics, electricity, blueprint reading, machine shop and physics.	Automotive mechanic, motor analyst, bakery, or refrigeration equipment, repairer, frame, wheel alignment and tractor mechanic.
Medical	Assists or supports physicians, surgeons, nurses, dentists, psychologists, social workers, and veterinarians in 29 separate job classifications. Some provide direct patient care in hospitals and clinics. Some make and repair eyeglasses, dentures, or orthomedical equipment, or maintain medical records.	Biology, chemistry, hygiene, sociology, general math, algebra, animal care; knowledge of mechanics or electronics; general clerical skills.	Social worker (case aide), practical nurse, nurse's aide, dental assistant, surgeon's assistant, psychological aide, hospital attendant or orderly, veterinary assistant, food quality control, medical equipment repairer, medical or dental laboratory technician, physical therapy assistant, occupational therapy assistant, and dietetic technician.
Military Intelligence	Gathers, translates, correlates and interprets information, including photographs, associated with military plans and operations.	English composition, typing, foreign languages, economics, geography and history.	Investigator, interpreter, cartographic aid, records analyst, research worker and intelligence analyst (government).
Petroleum	Receives, stores, preserves and distributes bulk packaged petroleum products; performs standard physical and chemical tests of petroleum products.	Hygiene, biology, physics, chemistry and mathematics.	Biological laboratory assistant, petroleum tester, chemical laboratory assistant.

Career Fields	Duties & Responsibilities	Qualifications	Examples of Civilian Jobs
Aircraft Maintenance	Performs the mechanical functions of maintenance, repair and modification of Marine air and ground support equipment.	Mechanical or electrical aptitude with manual dexterity, shop mathematics desirable.	Aircraft mechanic, electrician or hydraulics specialist; aviation machinist, sheet metal worker, aircraft instrument maker, repairer.
Airfield Services	Maintains aircraft log books, publications and flight operations records; prepares reports and schedules, installs and repairs aircraft launching and recovery equipment.	Typing, geography and mechanical drawing useful.	Airplane dispatch clerk, flight dispatcher, timekeeper and airport crash truck driver.
Air Traffic Control and Enlisted Flight Crews/Air Support/Anti-Air Warfare	Operates airfield control tower and radio-radar air traffic control systems; navigators, radio and radar operators and anti-air warfare missile batteryman.	Clear speaking voice, good hearing and better than average eyesight; speech, mathematics and electricity and experience as a radio ham helpful.	Airport control tower, or flight radio operator, navigator, instrument-landing truck operator, radio or television studio engineer.
Ammunition and Explosive Ordnance Disposal	Inspects, issues and supervises storage of ammunition and explosives; locates, disarms or detonates and salvages unexploded bombs.	Mechanics, general science, and chemistry useful.	Firearms and ammunition proof director, ordnance technician (government), powder and explosives inspector.
Auditing, Finance and Accounting	Prepares and audits personnel pay records, processes public vouchers and administers and audits unit fiscal accounts.	Computational work, arithmetic and attention to detail; typing, bookkeeping, office machines and mathematics useful.	Payroll or cost clerk, bookkeeper, cashier, bank teller, accounting and audit clerk and accountant.
Aviation Ordnance	Maintains and repairs aircraft armament systems, gun pods, machine guns, bomb racks and rocket/missile launcher equipment; assembles and loads bombs, rockets, guns and missiles; handles and stores aviation type munitions.	Electricity, hydraulics and mechanics shop courses useful.	Firearms assembler, gunsmith, armament mechanic and aircraft accessories repairer.
Avionics	Installs and repairs aircraft and aviation ground radio and radar equipment and systems, and air launched guided missiles; serves as electrician and instrument repairman, repairs flight instrument trainers.	Mathematics and shop courses in electricity, hydraulics and electronics useful.	Radio and television or electrical instrument repairer, communications, electrical or electronics engineer and radio operator.
Band	Performs in Marine Corps Band, unit bands and drum and bugle corps; repairs musical instruments.	Music experience as a member of a high school band or orchestra.	Musician, music librarian, music teacher, bandmaster, orchestra or music director and musical instrument repairer.
Engineer/ Construction Equipment and Shore Party	Performs metal-working, operation and maintenance of fuel storage areas, heavy engineering and pioneer equipment and construction and repairs of military facilities.	Automotive mechanics, sheet metal working machine shop, carpentry and mechanical drafting useful.	Sheet metal worker, engineering equipment mechanics, carpenter, road machinery operator, rigger and construction superintendent.
Data/ Communications Maintenance	Installs, inspects and repairs telephone, teletype and cryptographic equipment and cables, calibrates precision electronic, mechanical, dimensional and optical test instruments.	Mathematics, electricity and blueprint reading courses helpful.	Telephone installer and trouble shooter, radio repairer, cable splicer, and office machine serviceman.
Data Systems	Operates and programs data processing equipment	Clerical aptitude, manual dexterity and hand-eye coordination, mathematics, accounting and English useful.	Computer operator, programmer and data control coordinator
Drafting, Surveying and Mapping	Makes architectural and mechanical drawings, prepares military maps, makes topographic maps, creates or copies articles or illustrative materials.	Mathematics, mechanical drawing and drafting, geography and commercial art helpful.	Architectural or mechanical draftsman, surveyor or cartographer, geodetic computer, illustrator and commercial artist.

Career Fields	Duties & Responsibilities	Qualifications	Examples of Civilian Jobs
Electronics Maintenance	Installs, tests and repairs air-search radar, radio, radio relay, missile fire control and guidance systems.	Electronics, mathematics, electricity, electronics and blueprint reading useful.	Radio and television repair, radio engineer, electrical instrument repairer, recording, communications, and electrical engineer.
Food Service	Performs as cook, baker or meat cutter.	Hygiene, biology, chemistry, home economics and bookkeeping courses useful.	Cook, chef, baker, meat cutter or butcher, caterer, executive chef, dietician and restaurant manager.
Intelligence	Collects, records, evaluates and interprets information, makes detailed study of aerial photographs, conducts interrogations in foreign languages, translates written material and interprets conversations.	Geography, history, government, economics, English, foreign languages, typing, mechanical drafting and mathematics beneficial.	Investigator, research worker, intelligence analyst (government), map draftsman, cartographic aide and records analyst.
Legal Services	Prepares legal documents, operates stenotype machines.	Manual dexterity; English, filing, typing and shorthand desirable.	Law clerk, court reporter, chief clerk and stenotype operator.
Logistics	Performs administrative duties involving the supply, quartering, movement and transport of Marine units by land, sea and air.	Clerical aptitude, knowledge of verbal and math reasoning; operate mimeograph, ditto, adding and calculating machines, type 5-10 words a minute, read maps and understand simple filing procedures.	Inventory or shipping clerk, pier superintendent, stock control clerk or supervisor and warehouse manager.
Marine Corps Exchange and Clubs	Keeps and audits books and financial records, performs sales and merchandise stock control duties.	Typing, bookkeeping, business arithmetic, office machines and accounting useful.	Salesman, stock control supervisor, buyer, bookkeeper, accounting clerk, accountant and auditor.
Military Police and Corrections	Enforces military order, guards military and war prisoners and controls traffic.	Sociology and athletics helpful.	Policeman, ballistics expert and investigator.
Motor Transport	Performs auto mechanics and body repair, motor vehicles and amphibian truck operation.	Automotive mechanics, machine shop, electricity and blueprint reading useful.	Mechanic or automobile body, electrical systems repairer, truck driver, motor vehicle dispatcher, and motor transport depot master.
Nuclear, Biological and Chemical Warfare	Performs routine duties incident to applying detection, emergency and decontamination measures to gassed or radioactive areas. Inspects and performs preventive maintenance on chemical warfare protection equipment.	Must not have any known hypersensitivity to the wearing of protective clothing; be emotionally stable; biology and chemistry background beneficial.	Laboratory assistant (nuclear, biological or chemical), exterminator, decontaminator.
Operational Communications	Lays communication wire; installs and operates radio, radio telegraph and radio relay equipment; encodes and decodes messages.	Mathematics, typing, electricity and electronics useful.	Radio operator, telephone lineman, radio broadcasting traffic manager and communications engineer.
Ordnance	Inspects, maintains and repairs infantry, artillery, and anti-aircraft weapons; fire control optical instruments; operates machine tools or modifies metal parts.	Mathematics, mechanics, machine shop and blueprint reading, welding and heat treatment of metal and electricity.	Armament mechanic, gunsmith, time-recording equipment serviceman, tool and die maker, radio electrician, optical instrument inspector and electrical engineer.
Personnel and Administration	Performs as personnel classification clerk, administrative specialist and postal clerk.	Reasoning and verbal ability, and clerical aptitude. English composition, typing, shorthand and social studies helpful.	Secretary-typist, vocational advisor, employment interviewer, manager, office manager, job analyst and postal clerk.

Career Fields	Duties & Responsibilities	Qualifications	Examples of Civilian Jobs
Printing and Reproduction	Performs letterpress and lithographic offset printing. Sets type, operates linotype machines, presses, process cameras and bookbinding equipment.	General mathematics, printing and other graphic arts useful.	Printing compositor, linotype operator, photolithographer, pressman, printing bookbinder, printing plant makeup worker, proofreader, foreman.
Public Affairs	Gathers material for, writes and edits news stories, historical reports and gathers, prepares and edits radio and television broadcast scripts.	English grammar and composition, typing, speech and journalism courses helpful.	News reporter-correspondent, news rewrite man, columnist copyreader, copy or news editor, radio-television announcer and script writer.
Signals Intelligence/ Ground Electronic Warfare	Performs routine duties incident to collecting, translating, recording and disseminating information associated with military plans and operations.	English composition, geography and mathematics beneficial.	Radio intelligence operator, intelligence analyst, investigator and records analyst.
Supply Administration and Operations	Administration procurement, subsistence, packaging and warehousing; requisitions, purchases, receipts, accounts, classifies, stores, issues, sells, packages, preserves and inspects new, scrap, salvage, waste material, supplies and equipment.	Typing, bookkeeping, office machine operation and commercial subjects helpful.	Shipping, receiving, stock and inventory clerk, stock control supervisor, warehouse foreman-manager, parts man and purchasing agent.
Training and Audio-visual Support	Operates still, motion picture, and aerial cameras; develops film and prints photographs; repairs cameras and edits motion picture films. Performs as illustrator or draftsman.	Mathematics, chemistry and shop course in electricity. Normal color perception desirable.	Commercial illustrator, photographer, cinematographer, copy cameraman, motion picture film editor, camera and instrument repairer.
Transportation	Handles cargo and transacts business of freight shipping and receiving and passenger transportation.	Typing, bookkeeping, business arithmetic, office machine operation, and commercial subjects beneficial.	Shipping clerk, cargo handler, traffic rate clerk, freight traffic, passenger and railroad station agent.
Utilities	Installs, operates, and maintains electrical, water supply, heating, plumbing, sewage, refrigeration, hygiene and air conditioning equipment.	Mechanical aptitude and manual dexterity important. Vocational school shop courses in industrial arts and crafts beneficial.	Electrician, plumber, steam fitter, refrigeration mechanic, electric motor repairer and stationary engineer.
Weather Service	Collects, records and analyzes meteorological data; makes visual and instrumental observations and enters them on appropriate charts; forecasts short, intermediate and long range weather conditions.	Visual acuity correctable to 20/20, normal color perception; mathematics desirable, meterology and astronomy helpful.	Meteorologist, weather forecaster and observer.

Navy—Coast Guard

Career Fields	Duties & Responsibilities	Qualifications	Examples of Civilian Jobs
Aviation Anti-submarine Warfare Operator (Navy only) (C)	Performs general flight crew duties; operates ASW sensor systems, performs diagnostic function to effect fault, isolation and optimize system performance; operates tactical support center systems.	Above average learning ability. High degree of electrical and mechanical aptitude. Must pass flight physical and be able to swim. Courses in algebra, trigonometry, physics, electricity.	Radar technician, radio operator.

Career Fields	Duties & Responsibilities	Qualifications	Examples of Civilian Jobs
Electronic Warfare Technician (Navy only) (C)	Operates and maintains electronic countermeasures and electronic support measures, associated supporting equipment; evaluates, processes and applies intercept signal data, electronics intelligence reports, and electronic warfare tactics and doctrine to operational needs.	Prolonged attention and mental alertness. Physics, mathematics and courses in radio and electricity helpful, and experience in radio repair or ham radio. Normal sight and hearing, manual dexterity, and good memory.	Electronics technician, test equipment calibration technician.
Instrumentman (Navy only) (C)	Maintains, repairs mechanical instruments such as meters, gauges, office machines, watches and clocks.	Dexterity to do detailed work. Blueprint reading and practical experience in repairing office machines.	Watchmaker, instrument maker, typewriter serviceman, office machines mechanic, layout man.
Missile Technician (Navy only) (C)	Maintains Fleet ballistic missiles, and support and handling equipment, tests, adjusts, calibrates, operates, repair support handling equipment, handles/stows missiles.	High mechanical aptitude and manual dexterity. Electricity, electronics, mathematics, and physics.	Rocket engine component ordnance artificer.
Molder (Navy only) (C)	Operates foundries aboard ship and at shore stations; makes molds and cores, rigs flasks; casts ferrous, non-ferrous and alloy metals; sand-blasts castings and pours bearings.	Foundry, machine shop, practical mathematics.	Foundry foreman, furnace operator, melter, molder, core maker, heat treater, temperer.
Opticalman (Navy only) (C)	Maintains binoculars, sextants, optical gunsights, turret and marine periscopes.	Close, exact and painstaking workmanship. Physics, shop mathematics and machine shop helpful; experience in optical or camera manufacturing.	Lens grinder, jewelry stone cutter, tool inspector, instrument maker, inspector, optical tooling specialist, camera repairman and locksmith.
Patternmaker (Navy only) (C)	Makes wood, plaster and metal patterns, core boxes, flasks used by molders in Navy foundries.	Exacting, precise work. Woodshop, foundry, mechanical drawing, shop and practical mathematics.	Template maker, industrial arts teacher, layout man, patternmaker, form builder.
Aerographer's Mate (Navy only)	Collects, records, analyzes, meterological and oceanographic data; enters on appropriate charts; forecasts from visual and instrumental weather observations.	Algebra, geometry, trigonometry, physics, physiography, typing, training in meteorology and astronomy.	Weather observer, meteorological aide, chart maker, weather chart preparer.
Air Traffic Controller (Navy only)	Controls air traffic, operates radar air control ashore and afloat; uses radio, light signals; directs aircraft under visual flight and instrument flight conditions; assists in preparation of flight plans.	High degree of accuracy, precision, self-reliance and calmness under stress. Public speaking or experience in radio broadcasting.	Control tower operator, radio-telephone operator, airplane dispatch and aircraft log clerk.
Aircrew Survival Equipmentman (Navy) **Aviation Survivalman** (Coast Guard)	Maintains and packs parachutes, survival equipment, flight and protective clothing, life jackets; tests and services pressure suits. (Coast Guard: cares for search and rescue pyrotechnics and station small arms.)	Must perform extremely careful and accurate work. General shop and sewing desirable. Experience in use and repair of sewing machines	Parachute packer, inspector, repairer and tester; sailmaker.
Aviation Anti-Submarine Warfare Technician	Performs a wide range of electronic shop operations; performs in-flight maintenance of airborne electronic systems; removes and installs units of anti-submarine warfare equipment; debriefs flight crews; reads and applies service diagrams, schematics, and manuals; maintains operating efficiency of equipment; maintains inventory of required equipment, tools and materials; uses and maintains a variety of test equipment.	Arithmetic ability, manual dexterity, ability to do detailed work, a good memory, resourcefulness and curiosity.	Electronics mechanic.

Career Fields	Duties & Responsibilities	Qualifications	Examples of Civilian Jobs
Aviation Boatswain's Mate (Navy only)	Handles aircraft on carriers; operates, maintains, repairs aviation fueling, defueling, inert gas systems; maintains catapults, arresting gear.	20/20 vision uncorrected and good hearing. Shop work, physics and chemistry desirable. Experience in planes and hoisting equipment.	Machinery erector, crane operator, airport serviceman, gasoline distributor. Firefighter—crash fire and rescue.
Aviation Electrician's Mate	Maintains, adjusts, repairs aircraft electrical and instrument systems, plus power generating, lighting, electrical components of aircraft controls.	Algebra, trigonometry, physics and shop experience in aircraft electrical work.	Aircraft electrician, electrician, radio and TV repairer.
Aviation Electronics Technician	Tests, maintains, repairs aviation electronics equipment including navigation, identification, detection, reconnaissance, special purpose equipment; operates airborne electronic warfare equipment.	High degree of aptitude for electrical and mechanical work. Algebra, trigonometry, physics, electricity, radio and mechanics.	Aircraft electrician, radio mechanic, electrical repairer, instrument repairer, electronics technician, TV repairer.
Aviation Fire Control Technician (Navy only)	Maintains and inspects aircraft weapons systems, weapon-control radar, computers, computer sights, gyroscopes, related equipment; air launched guided missile equipment.	Superior electronic, electrical and mechanical aptitude. Training in repair shops or vocational schools and in mathematics.	Instrument man, airplane electrician, electronics technician, radar computer repairer, TV repairer.
Aviation Machinist's Mate	Inspects, maintains power plants and related systems and equipment; prepares aircraft for flight, conducts periodic aircraft inspections.	Good learning ability and mechanical aptitude. Machine shop, automobile or aircraft engine work, algebra and geometry.	Airport serviceman, aircraft engine test mechanic, small appliance repairer.
Aviation Maintenance Administrationman (Navy only)	Management and clerical duties in aircraft maintenance offices, plans and schedules maintenance workload, prepares reports and correspondence and analyzes trends of aircraft system and component failures.	Accurate and detailed work, has interest in the aviation maintenance field. Filing and typing.	Shipping, parts, supply room or maintenance clerk, office manager.
Aviation Ordnanceman (Navy only)	Loads bombs, torpedoes, rockets, guided missiles; maintains, repairs, inspects aircraft armament, aviation ordnance equipment.	Normal vision and good mechanical aptitude. Algebra, physics and electricity and experience in electrical or mechanical repair.	Gyroscope mechanic, instrumentman, ordnanceman, armament inspector.
Aviation Storekeeper (Navy only)	Receives, stores, issues aviation supplies, spare parts, technical aviation items; conducts inventories.	Bookkeeping, accounting, business arithmetic, typing and office practices.	Clerk typist, inventory, material, sales, or receiving/shipping clerk, accountant.
Aviation Structural Mechanic	Maintains, repairs aircraft, airframe, structural components, hydraulic controls, utility systems, egress systems.	High degree of mechanical aptitude. Metal shop, woodworking, algebra, plane geometry, physics; experience in automobile body work	Welder, sheet metal repairer, hydraulics technician, air conditioning repairer.
Aviation Support Equipment Technician (Navy only)	Services, tests and performs intermediate level maintenance and repair of gasoline and diesel engines, gas turbine compressor units, power generating equipment, liquid and gaseous oxygen and nitrogen servicing equipment, automotive electrical and air conditioning systems.	High mechanical aptitude. Mathematics, physics, electricity and machine shop and experience as auto mechanic or machinist.	Diesel or gasoline engine, air conditioning ignition mechanic, hydraulics repairer, auto mechanic.
Boatswain's Mate	Performs seamanship tasks, operates small boats, stores cargo, handles ropes and lines, directs works of deck force personnel.	Must be physically strong. Practical math skills desirable; algebra, geometry and physics.	Motorboat operator, pier superintendent, able seaman, canvas worker, rigger, cargo winchman, mate, longshoreman.
Boiler Technician (Navy) **Machinery Technician** (Coast Guard)	Operates boilers and fireroom machinery; transfers, tests and takes inventories of fuel and water; maintains boilers, pumps, associated machinery.	Strong interest in mechanical work. Shop courses and practical mathematics.	Marine fireman, boiler shop mechanic, boiler maker, stationary engineer, boiler or heating plant operator.

Career Fields	Duties & Responsibilities	Qualifications	Examples of Civilian Jobs
Builder (Navy only)	Constructs, maintains, repairs, wood, concrete, masonry structures; erects and repairs waterfront structures.	High mechanical aptitude. Carpentry and shop mathematics desirable. Experience with hand and power tools valuable.	Plasterer, roofer, mason, painter, construction worker, carpenter.
Construction Electrician (Navy only)	Installs, operates, maintains, repairs electrical generating and distribution systems, transformers, switchboards, motors, controllers.	Interest in mechanical and electrical work. Electricity, shop mathematics and physics helpful, ability to work aloft.	Powerhouse or construction electrician, electrical and telephone repairer.
Construction Mechanic (Navy only)	Maintains, repairs and overhauls automotive and heavy construction equipment.	High mechanical aptitude. Electrical or machine shop, shop mathematics and physics helpful. Machinist or auto mechanic work.	Automotive or diesel engine mechanic, motor analyst, construction equipment mechanic.
Cryptologic Technician (Navy only)	All prospective Cryptologic Technicians (CTs) must have a personal background that will facilitate clearance for special security access; above average speaking and writing ability; good memory; resourcefulness; curiosity; adaptability to detailed work; aptitude for math; record-keeping ability; ability to work well with others and manual dexterity.		
Cryptologic Technician A (Administrative)	Types messages and correspondence; files; handles classified material; keeps mail logs; prepares correspondence; orders supplies and takes inventory.	Exceptionally good character, speaking and writing ability.	Clerk typist, office manager.
Cryptologic Technician I (Interpretive)	Operates technical communications systems equipment; prepares data and reports involving communications material; performs temporary duty aboard submarines and surface units.	Foreign language aptitude.	Interpreter; translator.
Cryptologic Technician M (Maintenance)	Performs preventive and corrective maintenance on solid-state and electro-mechanical equipment which requires use of test equipment, hand tools and technical publications; repairs and calibrates wide variety of precision electronic test equipment.	Ability to comprehend advanced electronic theory.	Automatic equipment technician; central office repairer, radio mechanic.
Cryptologic Technician O (Communications)	Prepares messages utilizing teletypewriter equipment; transmits, receives, routes and logs message traffic; maintains message center files/logs and records; controls and operates communications equipment systems including radio receivers, tone-terminal equipment, DC and audio patch boards and communication security devices.	Typing ability, good memory, resourcefulness, curiosity, manual dexterity, aptitude for figures.	Cryptographic machines, telegraphic-teletypewriter operator.
Cryptologic Technician R (Collection)	Variety of duties associated with operation of teletype and morse communications systems; operates radio-receiving, direction-finding; and technical documents which are predominantly classified.	Good memory, speaking and writing ability.	Morse operator; radio officer.
Cryptologic Technician T (Technical)	Variety of duties associated with the operation of radio printer and other sophisticated equipment to study signal propagation; operates radio receiving, teletype, recording and related computer equipment; Morse code, security, communications procedures.	Above average speaking and writing ability, good memory.	Cryptanalyst; digital computer operator; electronic intelligence operations specialist and telegraphic-typewriter operator.
Data Processing Technician (Navy only)	Operates data processing equipment including sorters, collators, reproducers, tabulating printers and computers.	High clerical aptitude. Typing, bookkeeping and operating business machines desirable. Experience in mechanical work.	Data typist, key punch operator, systems analyst, verifier and tabulating machine operator.

Career Fields	Duties & Responsibilities	Qualifications	Examples of Civilian Jobs
Data Systems Technician (Navy only)	Maintains electronic digital data systems and equipment; inspects, tests, calibrates, and repairs computers, tape units, digital display equipment, data link terminal sets and related equipment.	Possess high aptitude for detailed mechanical work. Radio, electricity, physics, and mathematics through calculus.	Electrical, electronic repairer or computer repairer, electronic and data systems technician.
Dental Technician	Assists dental officers in treatment of patients; performs preventive procedures, and various dental department administrative duties.	Hygiene, physiology and chemistry.	Dental technician, dental hygienist, X-ray technician, dentist's assistant, dental laboratory technician.
Disbursing Clerk (Navy only)	Opens, maintains, closes military pay records; prepares reports and returns on public monies.	Typing, bookkeeping, accounting, business arithmetic and office practices.	Paymaster, cashier, statistical or audit clerk, bookkeeper, book-keeping machine operator, cost accountant.
Electronics Technician	Maintains all electronic equipment used for communications, detection ranging, recognition and counter-measures.	Aptitude for detailed mechanical work. Radio, electricity, physics, algebra, trigonometry and shop valuable.	Electronics technician, radar and radio repairer, instrument and electronics mechanic.
Electrician's Mate	Maintains power and lighting equip-ment, generators, motors, power distri-bution systems, other electrical equip-ment; rebuilds electrical equipment.	Aptitude for electrical and mechanical work. Electrical, practical and shop mathematics, and physics.	Electrician, electric motor and electrical equipment repairer, armature winder, radio/TV repairer.
Engineering Aid (Navy only)	Performs tasks required in construction surveying and drafting. Makes and controls surveys, runs and closes traverses; conducts soil classification and compac-tion tests.	Algebra, geometry, trigonometry, mechanical drawing and drafting recommended. Experience in road construction useful.	Surveyor, draftsman, soil analyst.
Engineman (Navy) **Machinery Technician** (Coast Guard)**	Operates, maintains, repairs internal combustion engines, main propulsion machinery, refrigera-tion and assigned auxiliary equipment.	Algebra, geometry and physics helpful. Experience in automotive repair.	Diesel engine operator, diesel mechanic, ignition repairer, small engine mechanic, marine oiler, stationary engineer.
Equipment Operator (Navy only)	Operates automotive and heavy construction equipment.	Good physical strength and normal color perception. Ex-perience in construction work, auto or electrical shop.	Bulldozer, pile driver, power shovel or motor grader operator, excavation foreman, truck driver.
Fire Control Technician	Operate, test, maintain and repair weapons control systems and telemetering equipment used to compute and resolve factors which influence accuracy of naval guns and missiles.	Perform fine, detailed work. Extensive training in mathematics, electronics, electricity and mechanics.	Radar or electronics technician, test range tracker, instrument repairer, electrician.
Gas Turbine System Technician (Navy only)	Operates gas turbine engines, main propulsion machinery and related electrical and electronic equipment.	Electrical/electronics repair, blueprint reading, mathematics and physics.	Electronics technician, gas turbine mechanic, power plant operator.
Gunner's Mate	Operate and perform maintenance on guided-missile launching systems, rocket launchers, guns, gun mounts; inspects/repairs electrical, electronic, pneumatic, mechanical and hydraulic systems.	Prolonged attention and mental alertness, ability to perform detailed work. High aptitude for electrical and mechanical work. Arithmetic, shop math, electricity, electronics, physics, machine shop, welding, mechanical drawing and shopwork.	Electronics technician, electrician, instrument repairer, hydraulics, pneumatic or mechanical technician, small appliance or test equip-ment repairer and ordnanceman.
Hospital Corpsman	Administers medicines, applies first aid, assists in operating room, nurses sick and injured.	Hygiene, biology, first aid, physiology, chemistry, typing and public speaking.	Practical nurse, medical or X-ray lab technician, nurse administrator.
Hull Maintenance Technician (Navy) **Damage Controlman** (Coast Guard)	Fabricates, installs, repairs ship-board structures, plumbing and piping systems; uses damage con-trol in firefighting, and nuclear, biological, chemical and radiological defense equipment.	High mechanical aptitude. Sheet metal, foundry, pipefitting, carpentry, mathematics, geometry and chemistry valuable.	Fireman, welder, plumber, shipfitter, blacksmith, metallurgical technician.

**All Navy engineering type rates are included in the Coast Guard Machinery Technician rating.

Career Fields	Duties & Responsibilities	Qualifications	Examples of Civilian Jobs
Illustrator Draftsman (Navy only)	Designs, sketches, does layout, letters signs, charts and training aids; operates visual presentation equipment; makes mathematical computations for layout and design illustrations.	Previous experience as draftsman, tracer or surveyor valuable. Art, mechanical drawing and blueprint reading valuable.	Structural draftsman, technical illustrator, specification writer, electrical draftsman, geodetic computer, graphic artist.
Intelligence Specialist (Navy only)	Maintains/uses intelligence files; prepares maps, graphics, mosaics, charts; extracts intelligence from aerial photos; prepares intelligence reports.	Processing, assimilating, interpreting and presenting data. Typing, filing, drafting, mathematics, geography and photography valuable.	Photographer, aerial picture analyst, chart maker, navigation instructor.
Interior Communications Electrician (Navy only)	Maintains, operates all interior communications systems, voice interior communications, alarms, ships control, plotting, automated propulsion equipment.	High aptitude for electrical work. Electrical shop, practical and shop mathematics, experience in electrical/electronics work desirable.	Powerhouse engineer, ship electrician, station installer, instrumentman, electronics or TV technician.
Journalist (Navy) Photojournalist (Coast Guard)	Reports, edits, copyreads news; publishes information about service people and activities through newspapers, magazines, radio and television.	High degree of clerical aptitude. English, journalism, typing and writing experience helpful.	News editor, copyreader, script writer, reporter, free lance writer, rewrite or art layout person, producer.
Legalman (Navy only)	Provides administrative services, military justice, claims, administrative law, and legal assistance; serves as court reporter.	Aptitude for detail, ability to express self in writing and orally. Typing, shorthand, English and logic helpful. No speech or hearing difficulties.	Legal assistant, law and contract clerk, title examiner and court reporter, office manager.
Lithographer (Navy only)	Performs offset lithography and letterpress printing, copy preparation, camera work, assembling and stripping, platemaking, typesetting, presswork and binding.	Work with machinery and chemicals. Printing, physics, chemistry, English and shop mathematics valuable.	Lithographic pressman, platen pressman, bookbinder, printer, photoengraver, cameraman, and photolithographer.
Machinery Repairman (Navy only)	Maintains assigned equipment to support other ships requiring use of milling machines, boring mills, other machine tools found in machine shops, overhaul and repair machinery.	Experience in practical or shop mathematics, machine shop, electricity, mechanical drawing and foundry desirable.	Engine lathe operator, machinist tool clerk, bench machinist, turret and milling machine operator and tool maker.
Machinist's Mate (Navy) Machinery Technician (Coast Guard)**	Operates, maintains and repairs ships' propulsion, auxiliary equipment and outside equipment such as steering engine, refrigeration/air conditioning, laundry equipment.	Aptitude for mechanical work. Practical or shop mathematics, machine shop, electricity and physics valuable.	Boiler house repairer, engine maintenance man, machinist, marine engineer, turbine operator, engine repairer, air conditioning and refrigeration repairer.
Marine Science Technician (Coast Guard only)	Makes visual/instrumental weather and oceanographic observations; conducts chemical analysis; enters data on appropriate logs, charts, and forms; analyzes/interprets weather and sea conditions.	Ability to use numbers in practical problems. Algebra, geometry, trigonometry, physics, physiography, chemistry, typing, meteorology, astronomy and oceanography useful.	Oceanographic technician, weather observer, meteorologist, chart maker, statistical clerk and inspector of weather and oceanographic instruments.
Master-at-Arms (Navy only)	Performs investigations, apprehensions, crime prevention, preservation of evidence; performs duties of beach guard and shore patrol, crowd control and brig operations.	Experience in police, shore patrol or investigative work. Maturity, good vision and hearing. High school diploma or equivalent.	Police officer, guard, detective, investigator.
Mess Management Specialist (Navy only)	Operates and manages Navy dining facilities and bachelor quarters; estimates quantities and kinds of foodstuffs required; receives, stows and breaks out food items; prepares menus; plans, prepares and serves meals; maintains stock records; conducts inventories; assists medical personnel in inspection for quality; complies with sanitary and hygienic requirements.	Experience or courses in food preparation, dietetics and record keeping helpful. High standards of honesty and cleanliness; good learning ability.	Caterer, cook, steward, chef, mess attendant, motel/hotel services assistant.

Career Fields	Duties & Responsibilities	Qualifications	Examples of Civilian Jobs
Mineman (Navy only)	Tests, maintains and repairs mines, components and mine laying equipment.	High mechanical aptitude. Electricity, machine shop work, welding, mechanical drawing and shop mathematics desirable.	Ordnanceman, mine assembler, ammunition foreman, powderman, electrician, harbor patrolman.
Musician	Provides music for military ceremonies, religious services, concerts, parades, various recreational activities; plays one or more musical instruments.	Proficiency on standard band or orchestral instruments.	Music teacher, instrument musician, orchestra leader, music arranger, instrument repairer, music librarian, arranger.
Navy Counselor (Navy only)	Organizes and implements enlisted recruiting and retention programs; counsels personnel and family members about career opportunities; maintains liaison with local media and gives presentations to civic groups.	E-5 eligible for E-6; ability to communicate effectively. Experience in guidance, teaching and courses in public speaking helpful.	Guidance counselor, social worker, recruiter.
Ocean Systems Technician (Navy only)	Operates special electronic equipment to interpret and document oceanographic data; operates related equipment such as tape recorders; interprets data; prepares and maintains visual displays of data; converts data into formats for statistical study.	Normal hearing, vision and color perception; above average learning ability; ability to perform detailed and repetitive work, to work harmoniously with others, and with numbers; and qualified for secret security clearance.	Computer-peripheral equipment operator or electronics technician.
Operations Specialist (Navy) Radarman (Coast Guard)	Operates surveillance and search radar, electronic recognition and identification equipment, controlled approach devices and electronic aids to navigation, serves as plotter and status board keeper.	Prolonged attention and mental alertness. Physics, mathematics and shop courses in radio and electricity helpful. Experience in radio repair or ham radio is valuable.	Radio operator (aircraft, ship government service, radio broadcasting), radar equipment foreman, and controlroom man, control tower operator.
Personnelman (Navy only)	Performs enlisted personnel administration duties in manpower utilization, maintains service records, personnel accounting, educational services, classifies personnel and jobs.	Ability to deal with people, typing, public speaking, office practices, personnel work and counseling helpful.	Employment manager, personnel clerk, vocational adviser, clerk typist, job or organizational analyst.
Photographer's Mate (Navy) Photojournalist (Coast Guard)	Operates, maintains and repairs cameras for ground and aerial photographic work.	Normal color perception; physics and chemistry desirable.	Photographer, camera repairer, aerial photographer.
Port Securityman (Coast Guard Reserve members only)	Supervises and controls the safe handling, transportation and storage of explosives and cargo. Responsible for security of vessels, harbors, waterfront facilities, fire extinguishment and prevention.	Normal hearing and vision; aptitude for mathematics, chemistry. Prior law enforcement experience beneficial.	Policeman, fireman, insurance investigator, warehouseman, pier superintendent.
Postal Clerk (Navy only)	Processes mail, sells stamps and money orders, maintains mail directories and handles correspondence concerning postal operations.	Bookkeeping, accounting, business arithmetic and typing helpful.	Parcel post or mail clerk, mail room manager, foreman, stock clerk, cashier.
Quartermaster	Performs navigation of ships, steering, lookout supervision, ship-control, bridgewatch duties, visual communication and maintenance of navigational aids.	Good vision and hearing and ability to express oneself clearly in writing and speaking. Public speaking, grammar, geometry and physics helpful.	Barge, motorboat, yacht captain, quartermaster, harbor pilot aboard merchant ships.
Radioman	Operates communication, transmission, reception, and terminal equipment; transmits, receives and processes all forms of military record and voice communications.	Good hearing and manual dexterity. Mathematics, physics and electricity desirable. Experience as amateur radio operator helpful.	Telegrapher, radio disptacher, radio/telephone operator, news copyman.

Career Fields	Duties & Responsibilities	Qualifications	Examples of Civilian Jobs
Religous Program Specialist (Navy only)	Assists in management of religious programs and facilities; trains volunteers; supervises the offices of chaplains; performs administrative duties.	Relate easily with people. Basic English, business arithmetic, typing, graphics and audio-visual familiarization useful.	Church business manager or administrator.
Sonar Technician	Operates electronic underwater detection and attack apparatus, obtains and interprets information for tactical purposes, maintains and repairs electronic underwater sound detection equipment.	Normal hearing and clear speaking voice. Algebra, geometry, physics, electricity and shopwork desirable. Experience as amateur radio operator.	Oil well sounding device operator, radio operator, inspector of electronic assemblies, electronic technician, electrical repairer.
Ship's Serviceman (Navy only)	Operates and manages ship's store activities afloat and ashore, including barber, cobbler, tailor, laundry, dry cleaning, soda fountains, commissaries, retail stores.	Shoe repairing, barbering, tailoring, merchandising and salesmanship, accounting, bookkeeping, business arithmetic and English helpful.	Barber, laundryman, dry cleaner, retail store manager, sales clerk, tailor, and shoe repairer.
Signalman (Navy only)	Sends and receives messages by flashing light, semaphore and flag hoist; handles, routes and files messages; codes and decodes message headings; operates voice radio; and maintains visual sight equipment.	Good vision and hearing, ability to express oneself clearly in writing and speaking.	Third mate, signalman, deck cadet, harbor policeman, small boat operator.
Steelworker (Navy only)	Fabricates, erects and dismantles pre-engineered structures, steel bridges and other structures. Lays out and fabricates steel and sheet metal; welds.	Physical strength, stamina and ability to work aloft. Sheet metal, machine shop, foundry experience desirable.	Rigger, shipfitter, structural steelworker, salvage engineer, steel fabricator, welder, sheet metal technician.
Storekeeper	Orders, receives, stores, inventories and issues clothing, foodstuffs, mechanical equipment and other items. In the Coast Guard also performs duties as Navy disbursing clerk.	Typing, bookkeeping, accounting, commercial arithmetic, general business studies and English helpful.	Sales or shipping clerk, warehouseman, buyer, invoice control clerk, purchasing agent.
Subsistence Specialist (Coast Guard only)	Cooks and bakes, prepares menus, keeps cost accounts, assists in ordering provisions, inspects foodstuffs.	Experience or courses in food preparation, dietetics, and record keeping helpful.	Cook, pastry chef, steward, pie maker, butcher, chef, baker.
Telephone Technician (Coast Guard only)	Installs, operates, maintains and repairs all telephone, telegraph and teletype equipment, switchboards, public address systems and inter-office communications systems.	Aptitude for electrical and mechanical work, use of numbers in practical problems. Previous electrical experience helpful.	Electrician, electricial equipment inspector and many jobs which are in the civilian field of telephonic communications.
Torpedoman's Mate (Navy only)	Maintains and overhauls torpedoes and depth charges; maintains and repairs ordnance launching equipment; launches and recovers torpedoes.	High mechanical and electrical aptitude. Electricity, machine shop, welding, mechanical drawing and shop mathematics desirable.	Ordnance foreman, gyroscope assembly supervisor, instrument mechanic, electronics technician, motor/ office machine repairer.
Tradevman (Navy only)	Operates, maintains, installs, repairs training aids and training devices; maintains audio/visual training aids.	Mathematics, physics, electricity, shop work experience and instructor experience desirable.	Electronics technician, instructor, flying/pilots instructor, radio mechanic.
Utilitiesman (Navy only)	Installs, maintains, repairs and codes plumbing, heating systems, steam, compressed air, fuel storage, collection and disposal facilities and water purification units.	High mechanical aptitude. Apprentice training in plumbing and related fields, mathematics helpful.	Stationary engineering assistant, plumber, pipe fitter, water plant or boiler operator, boiler house foreman, pumpman.
Yeoman	Clerical and secretarial, typing, filing, operating office and duplicating equipment, preparing and routing correspondence and reports, maintains records and official publications.	Same qualifications required of secretaries and typists in private industry; English, business subjects, stenography and typewriting helpful.	Office manager, secretary, general office clerk, administrative assistant.

6. Education And Training Opportunities

The world's largest school has neither a football team nor a homecoming queen, but it does have over a million students enrolled in a variety of courses that qualify people in hundreds of vocational skills. Also, this school enables thousands each year to receive college degrees and other advanced training certification. The name of the school: the United States Armed Forces.

The one great feature of the training and education provided by the armed forces "school" is that it's all free, and the students attend classes during the work day!

You've seen in the last chapter the many job opportunities available in the armed forces. For each of these jobs, people must be trained. To accomplish this, the military operates the largest training system in the world. All the schools in the Big Ten Football Conference don't rival it in size. Even all the colleges in a large state like Texas don't come close to matching the breadth and extent of the military's vast training system. It is a training system that includes hundreds of technical schools and thousands of college courses offered at over 650 education and learning centers around the globe.

How good is the military's education programs? Well, you might ask Lieutenant Colonel Paul Murphey of the 351st Strategic Missile Wing, Whiteman AFB, Colorado. Lt. Col. Murphey now has a Ph.D., yet he joined the Navy in 1956 as a high school dropout! Murphey's test scores were high so he applied to the Naval Academy. He was accepted for the Naval Academy Prep School, which qualified him for an appointment to the Academy. Graduating from there in 1962, he was commissioned a second lieutenant in the Air Force. Later, while in service, he earned both a master's degree and a doctorate.

The remarkable achievements of Lt. Col. Murphey are unusual, but he demonstrates what a young person can accomplish in the military with dedication and desire. Armed with these two traits, you can attain your own goals while in service.

IN SUPPORT OF THE MISSION

Training and education support the mission of the armed forces in several ways. First, it prepares the individual to perform the job for which he enlisted and thus helps the service to meet its national defense commitment; second, it helps individuals mature and be more effective; and, finally, it helps people to achieve personal goals and become a more productive part of the military team. The military spends billions to further these aims, and our leaders feel that it's money well spent.

What can you personally get from the military's commitment to training and education? Four things:

- Technical school training
- Apprenticeship or on-the-job training
- Continuation training
- College credits or a degree

Each of these deserves comment.

Technical School Training

After boot camp, most persons will report to a military technical school to be trained initially in their chosen career field or occupational specialty. Each of the services operates a huge network of technical training schools that provides this training.

Technical schools in the military are so highly thought of that many civilian colleges, schools, and universities across the nation give college credit if you have completed a military technical training course. Accrediting agencies have deemed the Air Force's enlisted technical schools so effective in curriculum and instruction that the service schools were given full, transferable credit. As a result, the Congress established the two-year Community College of the Air Force (CCAF). By completing many Air Force courses, you are simultaneously receiving documented college courses. The CCAF is authorized to award associate degrees in a number of majors.

Military schools are considered by many civilian authorities to be far superior to civilian vocational colleges. Our nation's very existence depends on how well you—and thousands of other incoming servicepeople—learn your jobs. Technical schools are the place where this learning starts.

You should know, also, that the military schools often start from scratch; that is, they begin with the very basics of knowledge and go from there to teach people complex tasks and skills. So if you are worried that you can't learn a seemingly complex skill in electronics, mechanics, or another field, set your worries aside. The service will train you even if you have had no prior training in the subject in which you are interested.

Some examples of the courses taught in service technical schools are:

Army:
Radar
Satellite Communications
Data Processing
Medical Administration
Vehicle Maintenance
Missile Mechanic

Air Force:
Aircraft Maintenance
Teletype Repair
Avionics
Disaster Preparedness
Security Police
Air Traffic Control

Coast Guard: Legal Assistant
Personnel
Postal
Steelwork
Signals
Machinist

Navy: Data Systems Technician
Motion Picture Equipment Repair
Sonar Technician
Interior Electrician
Dental Technician
Aviation Ordinance

Marine: Aviation Structure Mechanic
Air Control
Photography
Weather Observation/Aerography
Airborne Radio Operator
Intelligence

Apprenticeship or On-the-Job Training

Some persons go straight to their first job after boot camp. There they begin an apprenticeship or on-the-job training (OJT) program. However, even those who arrive at their first job after technical school must still be trained on their specific duties. They also begin an apprenticeship or OJT program.

Your superior in your first job assignment won't expect you to know everything about how to do your job. He'd be shocked if you did. All he wants is for you to agree to do your best to learn, a step at a time. As you learn, your progress will be documented. Eventually you'll be tested on what you know, and when you have finally achieved skilled status, you'll receive appropriate certification.

This certification could be valuable. It lets civilian employers know you have passed a thorough learning program and are fully qualified at your occupation. Some colleges and vocational schools will give you free credit or advanced standing in classes based on your military skill certification.

The Army has arranged with the U.S. Department of Labor a terrific apprenticeship program. The Army logs in evidence of your training. When you've finally reached the point where you can be called a journeyman, you'll receive a Certificate of Completion of Apprenticeship from the Department of Labor. In some skills, however, your short time in the Army won't be enough to qualify you for the certificate. In that case, the hours you've logged and the experience you've gained will be documented for potential employers so you'll have an impressive record to show when you're job hunting.

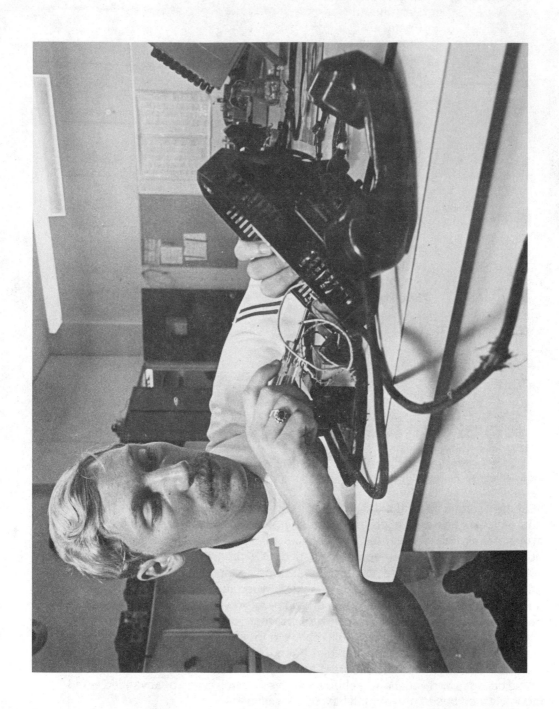

Continuation Training

The services recognize that in today's world of rapidly changing technology you must keep abreast of new ideas and knowledge in your field. Therefore, they've come up with an impressive system of short courses you can take to improve your skills after your initial training is over. For instance, a helicopter-engine repairer may be sent to a technical school course to learn how to repair a new helicopter that is just coming into the inventory. Or an aircraft specialist may be sent to learn the newest techniques to prevent frame corrosion.

Another way the services help you to stay up-to-date and also to broaden your knowledge are their correspondence school courses. The Army's Institute for Professional Development (AIPD) and the Air Force's Extension Course Institute (ECI) are two examples. Each permits you to take any of a large number of correspondence courses. Both the AIPD and ECI are recognized by the National Home Study Council; and the American Council on Education has recommended college credit for many of their courses.

An incredible number of courses are offered. The AIPD alone offers 995 correspondence courses. These include courses in military police, field artillery, signal, and air defense. The ECI courses include legal services, administration, fire protection, automotive repair, and radio repair. You can take one of these courses (they're free!) even if you are assigned to a different career field than that covered in the course.

College Credits or a Degree

The services are big on education also. While training prepares you for your military job and helps you to stay abreast of new developments in your field, education broadens your horizons, so to speak, and improves your knowledge of important subjects. Education makes you a well-rounded person, flexible, and more able to meet everyday challenges.

At practically every military installation, education courses are conducted on a continuing and frequent basis. Typically, these are college classes, but high school preparation courses are also offered as well as classes designed to improve your language and mathematics skills. Military supervisors do their best to arrange work schedules so you can attend these courses in your off-duty hours. Occasionally you may be given time off to attend.

These courses are voluntary, but if you attend, the service may pay 75 percent, 90 percent, or all of the cost of books, fees, and tuition. That's true even if they're taught by a civilian college or institution, as many are.

The military has arrangements with a great number of colleges and universities that allow these institutions to use military facilities to hold classes. Such schools as the University of Maryland, Park College, Western Kentucky University, North Carolina State, University of Southern California, Pepperdine, and many others offer courses on military stations under this cooperative arrangement.

Even being stationed overseas or sea duty doesn't have to deter you from furthering your college education. These colleges offer courses aboard ships and at scores of locations overseas. Whether your goal is simply a course or two to add interest to your life, an associate or bachelor's degree, or even a doctorate, the services are doing everything they can to help you.

Importantly, these schools are liberal in granting transfer credits, so if you leave one station to go to another, you can transfer your credits to the new college. The services have worked hard to set up a transfer-of-credits program and, today, hundreds of junior, community, and four-year colleges have agreed to allow transfer of credits for military personnel. This is in recognition of the fact that servicepeople are mobile and often must change stations every year or two due to no fault of their own.

The Army even has one program—Project AHEAD—that allows you to select a college at the time you enlist as your "home campus." Therefore, as you go from post to post, taking college courses from a number of different schools, you can rest assured that your "home campus" will accept the credits earned as if you were actually attending the college. The Navy has a similar program, called the Navy Campus for Achievement (NCFA).

The Air Force, of course, has its own community college (CCAF), which will document your credits earned while in service and give you an official college transcript. CCAF awards four hours of college credit in physical education and first aid for your attending basic training, so you start out with four semester hours on your transcript.

Testing Out

One way to get college credits without actually attending classes is to "test out." You can test out by taking an exam designed to test your knowledge in a specific college course or area. If you make a minimum acceptable score, you can receive college credit. The amount of hours awarded is at the discretion of the university or college to which you apply.

The CLEP (College Level Examination Program) general test is the best known of these tests. By taking and passing the CLEP you can be awarded up to 30 semester hours—one full year—of college credit. Yet you need not spend one day in an actual class. Civilians can also take the CLEP, but they must pay for the privilege. You don't.

Also, there are CLEP subject exams which test your knowledge in a specific course area: English, algebra, world history, foreign languages, etc. The services themselves offer a similar, in-house testing program called DANTES (Defense Activity for Non-traditional Education Support). DANTES tests are also available in a variety of subject areas, are free to servicepeople, and can result in the awarding of college credits. Civilians are not eligible to take DANTES tests.

EDUCATION CENTERS

To help you reach your educational goals, the services have established an education center or office on practically every installation. These centers are staffed with trained counselors and staff who are there to assist the members of the installation. They coordinate programs with local universities, make their facilities available for testing and the conduct of courses, and otherwise plan and administer an effective education program.

As soon as you arrive at your first permanent duty post, drop in at your education center, talk to a counselor, and learn the many programs the center offers. If you really want training and education, you're in the right place when you join the military.

7. Where Will You Be Assigned?

Travel! Adventure! People and places! That's what the military offers you. You name the country and there's a good chance that American servicepeople are either stationed there or visit by ship or submarine on occasion. The lure of seeing new, sometimes exotic foreign lands is a primary reason why many join the service. A recent Department of Defense (DOD) study revealed that 21 percent of those polled gave "travel" as their reason for choosing the military.

But foreign lands aren't the only travel destinations you can reach in the military. There are hundreds of "nooks and crannies" in the United States itself where you may be assigned—for example, near metropolitan areas like San Diego, California; Orlando, Florida; Washington, D.C.; and Austin, Texas. And there are the little "burgs" like New London, Connecticut; Point Mugu, California; Winter Harbor, Maine; and Fallon, Nevada. Altogether, there are over 250 major base posts and stations in the United States and hundreds of small sites and installations. So, as you can see, whether you opt for overseas or the good old U.S., the possibilities are virtually endless.

Your opportunity to travel is great, regardless of which service you join. Of course, Coast Guard assignments overseas are more limited than those available to soldiers and airmen, but even that service has some installations in foreign locations.

WHERE MILITARY PEOPLE ARE

According to current DOD figures, nearly a half million military people are stationed overseas. That's almost 25 percent of everyone in uniform. Here's how it breaks down by region and country:

Europe (330,000)

West Germany	234,300
Great Britain	22,300
Italy	12,100
Spain	8,800
Turkey	4,800
Greece	3,700
Iceland	2,800
Netherlands	2,200

Belgium	2,000
Portugal	1,400
Other Countries	800
Sixth Fleet	34,800

The Pacific and the Far East (138,300)

Japan and Okinawa	45,900
South Korea	41,600
Philippines	14,400
Guam	8,400
Taiwan	800
Australia	700
Midway	400
Other Countries	200
Seventh Fleet	25,900

Latin America (15,900)

Panama Canal Zone	9,200
Puerto Rico	4,000
Guantanamo	2,300
Other	400

Other Areas (10,000)

Bermuda	1,300
Diego Garcia	1,200
Canada	700
Saudi Arabia	400
Other	2,100
Naval Forces Afloat	400

As you can see, Western Europe is the major region where you might be assigned. About two-thirds of all U.S. servicemen and women overseas are in Europe, in countries like Germany, Britain, Italy, and Spain. In these nations, we have forces that are ready for action in the event communist forces attack from the East. These forces include huge naval installations in Livorno, Italy, and Rota, Spain; Army camps in Wiesbaden, and Frankfurt, West Germany; and air bases near Venice, Italy, and in Amsterdam, the Netherlands.

The benefits of spending a tour in Europe are obvious. The Coliseum in Rome, the Eiffel Tower in Paris, and the Tower of London all beckon you. However, don't underrate the attractions of the Orient. Thousands of servicemen and women have sampled the bustle of Tokyo and Seoul, the quaint villages of Taiwan, and the rugged back country of Australia.

BETTER THAN TOURING

If you are fortunate enough to be assigned permanently in a foreign country for one year, or even up to four years, you'll be able to see and do things that are only dreamed of by the average tourist. The quick and hurried glance that tourists get of faraway lands cannot compare with the reward you'll get as you discover and feel the ordinary people on a daily basis. You'll share the inside life of the people and learn the culture. Tourists often pay thousands of dollars for a mere peek; you'll have an in-depth and envious living experience, and it won't cost you a cent!

An added benefit of being assigned overseas is the existence of Armed Forces Recreation Centers (AFRCs). AFRCs are recreational centers located in outstanding scenic vacation areas. All servicepeople and their dependents are eligible to use these facilities. The AFRCs offer either cut-rate or reasonably priced food and beverages, lodging, and exceptional recreational activities. Outdoor activities include snow skiing, swimming, scuba, boating, diving, golf, and tennis. Some of the more popular AFRCs are at Garmisch, Berchtesgaden, Chiemsee, and Munich in Germany; Hale Koa in Hawaii; and Seward, Alaska.

By the way, there are also AFRCs located at many sites within the United States. Again, the only requirement for their use is that you be an armed forces member.

TOUCH AND GO

Even if you can't stay—if perhaps you are a seaman on a Navy ship that on its cruises takes in a number of seaports, or you are assigned to an airplane squadron that spends only a few weeks overseas at a time—you'll be the envy of millions of civilians. After all, think of all the people in the U.S. who never get the chance to leave their backyard or home state, let alone take in the glamorous and interesting sights in Europe, Japan, and elsewhere. Not so the average serviceperson.

In some ways, sailors and Marines have it even better than their Army and Air Force counterparts. Some ships and vessels take annual cruises to a number of ports. For instance, a Navy cruiser whose home port is San Diego, California, may sail for three months out of the year, with short stopovers in a number of Latin American docks—Panama, Costa Rica, Venezuela, and Chile. Other ships and carriers make Mediterranean, Pacific, and European-Atlantic tours.

TOUR LENGTH

When you go overseas, the period of time you must stay at a particular station is called a tour. For instance, the tour for a married soldier in Germany, accompanied by family, is 36 months. The tour for an unaccompanied airman in Spain is two years. The tour length varies by location and whether or not a service member opts to take his family on the tour.

Length of tour varies by location, depending on the austerity of the local conditions. A tour in remote Greenland, a site snowed in most of the year and where dependents are prohibited, is a mere twelve months, whereas a tour to a more plush area such as Hawaii or England is usually three years for accompanied members or two years for singles and unaccompanied persons.

YOUR CHANCES

What are your chances of assignment to a foreign country? It depends. If you plan to enlist in the Army, you might inquire about that branch's guaranteed assignment enlistment option. If you qualify and there is an opening where you want to go, you will be guaranteed assignment to Europe, Hawaii, Panama, Alaska, or somewhere in the United States. At the time this book went to press, none of the other services offered a guaranteed overseas assignment program like the Army's, but they did have a base-of-choice option for the continental United States.

Even though you may not be guaranteed an overseas slot, usually the military services do their best to accommodate volunteers. You will have an opportunity, either at the AFES recruiting station, in boot camp, or during technical training, to ask for your choice of assignments for both the U.S. and overseas. You will also have the opportunity to request a specific unit or Navy/Coast Guard vessel.

In years past, volunteer requests were only dimly considered. This is why the forms that a military person filled out to volunteer for his area, base, and unit of choice were called "dream sheets." As one Air Force lieutenant said to me, "I put down on my dream sheet at Officer Training School that I wanted to go to Travis Air Force Base in California. Instead, I was sent to Pope Air Force Base in North Carolina! Either the personnel guy didn't know the difference between the West and East or he got his oceans mixed up."

Nowadays, the military uses computers to track assignments. There's no personnel guy to get "mixed up." This isn't to say that everyone gets sent where he wants to go. Far from it. There are some very unattractive military posts where no one wants to be assigned. Obviously *someone* has to go there. For instance, the U.S. has a small peacekeeping force in the Sinai Desert in Egypt. Few volunteer for this harsh duty. Still, a U.S. contingent is needed there. Hopefully, you won't be the unfortunate soul who gets assigned to a place that many consider "the end of the earth."

The best way for you to get the assignment of your choice is to communicate your desires every chance you get. Tell the recruiter, the guidance counselor at the AFES, the personnel clerks during boot camp, and the assignments personnel at your technical school base or post. If your first asssignment is to some place other than your first choice, don't give up hope. When you arrive at your first post, do your job in an excellent manner, but continue to communicate your desire to go to Germany, to Plattsburgh, New York, or wherever. The services are not as bureaucratic and impersonal as many make them out to be. The personnel clerks *are* human and they will understand your sincere desires and will do their best to see you get what you want, whenever possible.

FOR LOVERS OF HOME

All this talk about the thrill and pleasures of overseas duty, and yet I'll bet there are many of you reading this book that aren't interested in the least in leaving the homeland. Traveling outside the confines of the U.S.A. doesn't interest you at all. If this describes your feelings, then you are probably in luck.

Chances are that your first assignment in the military will be somewhere in the United States. Foreign duty is mainly for volunteers, career people, and those who have a few years experience under their belt. The services have learned that older, more mature persons and volunteers perform best in an overseas environment. For Coast Guard members, a stateside assignment is almost a cinch.

Still, there's no certainty (except for those who enlist under the guaranteed-station option) that you'll be allowed to stay in Uncle Sam's territory. And if you're a member of the Navy, your ship or submarine may alternate between sea duty and shore time. Anyway, you might just be surprised how much you will enjoy the sights overseas if not the scenery or the cosmopolitan cities, then perhaps that pretty, blue-eyed *fraulein* in Berlin or, for you ladies, that handsome Italian fellow in Rome. There's always both advantages and disadvantages in everything, right?

TAKING YOUR FAMILY

Like any American, you have a right to take your wife or husband and your children along with you on an assignment. Of course, you should carefully consider the expenses involved before you decide to have your family accompany you.

During your first year or so, you may find it impossible or impractical to have your family moved to your new assignment. This is because you'll undoubtedly be moving frequently. First, there's boot camp, then perhaps a training course or two or even three. And this training will rarely be conducted at a single base; it may be given at different locations that are far apart.

Separation from your family can be tough, but there is an advantage. You can devote more time to training, learning new skills, and getting settled in your new job and first assignment.

The most serious obstacle married recruits face is moving their families to their first permanent duty station. Enlisted persons with two years or less of service are not paid by the government to move their dependents. The entire burden of moving falls on the shoulder of the individual. It's hard enough on E-1, E-2, or E-3 pay to afford moving a household from one place to another in the United States. But overseas? For a young person with a family, the cost of having his family join him in the foreign country is just plain out of the question.

Another problem is a job for the spouse. Over 52 percent of American wives must work to help maintain their family's standard of living. Unfortunately, few jobs are available for the spouse in foreign nations, or in U.S. communities where residence for servicepeople is temporary and often fleeting. No one wants to hire a person who, several months or so down the pike, must uproot and leave, forcing the employer to seek a new replacement.

Don't forget the problem of housing, either. Typically, the military service does not have enough housing units to accommodate E-4's with less than two years' service. Rightly or wrongly, military housing is usually reserved for career people and their families. And as for "living on the economy," rent in some countries is so outrageous that young service families have to live in substandard housing, at inflated prices, that could only be termed ghettos back home.

If you do decide to have your family accompany you, be sure to carefully study the financial impact before you make the move. It might save you a lot of unnecessary stress and financial hardship.

A LISTING OF MILITARY INSTALLATIONS

Here's a by-service list of military bases, posts, and stations where you might be assigned in the United States, and a current rundown on the countries overseas where the services have larger installations (Coast Guard omitted). The military population of the installation is shown in parenthesis after each listing to give you an idea of your chances for assignment. Only stations with at least 300 personnel assigned are listed. Note that Alaska, Hawaii, and Puerto Rico are considered overseas tour areas by the Department of Defense.

Army—Stateside

Alabama:	Fort McClellan (9,000); Redstone Arsenal (3,500); Fort Rucker (7,511).
Alaska:	Fort Greely (800); Fort Richardson (4,610); Fort Wainwright (2,700).
Arizona:	Fort Huachuca (6,331); Yuma Proving Ground (533).
California:	Fort Hunter (1,100); Fort Ord (20,800); Presidio of Monterey (2,500); Presidio of San Francisco (2,950); Sierra Army Depot (350).
Colorado:	Fort Carson (21,000); Fitzsimmons Army Medical Center (1,900).
District of Columbia:	Fort Lesley J. McNair (900); Walter Reed Army Medical Center (2,800).
Georgia:	Fort Benning (22,887); Fort Gillem (see Fort McPherson); Fort Gordon (19,866); Hunter Army Airfield (3,500); Fort McPherson (includes Fort Gillem) (1,985); Fort Stewart (14,685).
Hawaii:	Schofield (15,000); Fort Shafter (1,010); Tripler Army Medical Center (1,600).
Illinois:	Fort Sheridan (1,400).
Indiana:	Fort Benjamin Harrison (3,900).
Kansas:	Fort Leavenworth (3,000); Fort Riley (19,600).
Kentucky:	Fort Campbell (21,271); Fort Knox (19,200).
Louisiana:	Fort Polk (13,316).
Maryland:	Aberdeen Proving Ground (includes Edgewood Arsenal) (5,300); Fort Detrick (738); Fort George G. Meade (11,125); Fort Ritchie (1,108).
Massachusetts:	Fort Devens (6,100).
Missouri:	Fort Leonard Wood (15,000).
New Jersey:	Fort Dix (3,563); Fort Monmouth (1,524).
New Mexico:	White Sands Missile Range (1,413).
New York:	Fort Drum (700); Fort Hamilton (includes Fort Totten) (1,950); Seneca Army Depot (500); U.S. Military Academy (2,000).

North Carolina:	Fort Bragg (37,800).
Oklahoma:	Fort Sill (22,535).
Pennsylvania:	Carlisle Barracks (509); New Cumberland Army Depot (428).
South Carolina:	Fort Jackson (16,000).
Texas:	Fort Bliss (25,000); Fort Hood (39,934); Fort Sam Houston (10,485).
Utah:	Dugway Proving Ground (2,700).
Virginia:	Fort A. P. Hill (see Fort Lee); Arlington Hall Station (649); Fort Belvoir (6,300); Cameron Station (445); Fort Eustis (8,625); Fort Lee (includes Forts Pickett, A. P. Hill)—Lee (7,707), Pickett (500), A. P. Hill (340); Fort Monroe (1,200); Fort Myer (4,000); Fort Pickett (see Fort Lee); Vint Hill Farms (600).
Washington:	Fort Lewis (20,600).

Army—Overseas

Alaska	Okinawa
Belgium	Panama
Germany	Philippines
Hawaii	Puerto Rico
Italy	Thailand
Japan	Turkey
Korea	Great Britain

Navy—Stateside

Alaska:	Adak NS (2,200).
California:	Alameda NAS (2,600); China Lake Naval Weapons Center (830); Concord Naval Weapons Station (550); Coronado Naval Amphibious Base (3,500); Lemoore NAS (4,700); Long Beach Naval Regional Medical Center (620); Long Beach NS (10,000); Mare Island Naval Complex (3,000); Miramar NAS (10,000); Moffett Field NAS (5,500); Naval Postgraduate School (812); North Island NAS (30,000); Oakland Naval Regional Medical Center (1,400); Point Mugu Pacific Missile Test Center (928); Port Hueneme Naval Construction Battalion Center (4,000); San Diego Naval Regional Medical Center (2,500); San Diego NS (36,000); Treasure Island NSA (3,050).
Connecticut:	New London NSB (14,150).
District of Columbia:	Naval Security Station (650); Washington Navy Yard (1,600).
Florida:	Cecil Field NAS (6,963); Corry Station (3,000); Jacksonville NAS (9,671); Key West NAS (2,558); Mayport NS

(14,000); Orlando Naval Training Center (2,500); Pensacola Naval Aerospace and Regional Medical Center (716); Pensacola NAS (12,000); Whiting Field NAS (2,500).

Georgia: Atlanta NAS (600); Kings Bay NSB (2,000); Navy Supply Corps School (350).

Hawaii: Barbers Point NAS (2,200); Pearl Harbor NB (23,000); Wahiawa Naval Communication Area Master Station, Eastern Pacific (1,096).

Idaho: Idaho Falls Naval Nuclear Power Training Unit (1,500).

Illinois: Glenview NAS (1,000); Great Lakes NB (30,000).

Louisiana: New Orleans NAS (715); New Orleans NSA (2,000).

Maine: Brunswick NAS (3,800); Winter Harbor Naval Security Group Activity (300).

Maryland: Annapolis NS (350); Bethesda National Naval Medical Center (1,889), Indian Head Naval Ordnance Station (500); Patuxent River NAS (3,400); U.S. Naval Academy (1,377).

Massachusetts: South Weymouth NAS (300).

Mississippi: Gulfport Naval Construction Battalion Center (4,093); Meridian NAS (2,330).

Nevada: Fallon NAS (550).

New Hampshire: Portsmouth Naval Shipyard (120 permanent active duty—average 1,000 active duty in port).

New Jersey: Lakehurst Naval Air Engineering Center (900).

New York: Ballston Spa (see Scotia Navy Depot); Mitchell Housing Annex (622); Scotia Navy Depot (includes Ballston Spa) (2,200).

Pennsylvania: Philadelphia NB (3,000); Willow Grove NAS (2,000).

Rhode Island: Newport Naval Education and Training Center (3,350).

South Carolina: Charleston NB (23,600).

Tennessee: Memphis NAS (13,000).

Texas: Chase Field NAS (1,700); Corpus Christi NAS (2,800); Dallas NAS (1,300); Kingsville NAS (1,700).

Virginia: Dam Neck Fleet Combat Training Center, Atlantic (4,000); Little Creek Naval Amphibious Base (3,900); Norfolk NB (89,000); Oceana NAS (9,000); Yorktown Naval Weapons Station (700).

Washington: Bangor NSB (2,243); Bremerton Naval Regional Center (356); Puget Sound Naval Shipyard (5,250); Seattle NSA (1,843); Whidbey Island NAS (6,264).

Navy—Overseas

Alaska	Japan
Bermuda	Korea
Cuba	Panama
Guam	Puerto Rico
Hawaii	Philippines
Iceland	Spain
Italy	United Kingdom

Marine Corps—Stateside

Arizona:	Yuma MCAS (3,500).
California:	Barstow MC Logistics Base (900); El Toro MCAS (10,700); Camp Pendleton (33,000); San Diego MC Recruit Depot (2,300); Tustin MCAS (Helicopter) (2,375); Twentynine Palms (6,500).
District of Columbia:	Marine Barracks (1,000).
Georgia:	Albany MC Logistics Base (1,136).
Hawaii:	Kaneohe MCAS (9,000); Camp H. M. Smith (1,800).
Missouri:	Kansas City MC Finance Center (600).
North Carolina:	Cherry Point MCAS (15,000); Camp Lejeune (33,000); New River MCAS (Helicopter) (4,700).
South Carolina:	Beaufort MCAS (3,589); Parris Island MC Recruit Depot (2,650).
Virginia:	Henderson Hall (350); Quantico MC Development and Education Command (7,800).

Marine Corps—Overseas

Alaska	Japan
Bermuda	Korea
Cuba	Panama
Guam	Puerto Rico
Hawaii	Philippines
Iceland	Spain
Italy	United Kingdom

Coast Guard—Stateside

Alabama:	Mobile Aviation Training Center (400).
Alaska:	Kodiak USCG Support Center (700).
California:	Alameda CG Training Center (300).
Connecticut:	U.S. Coast Guard Academy (1,001).
Maryland:	Curtis Bay (380).
Massachusetts:	Otis CG Air Station—Cape Cod (300).
New Jersey:	Cape May CG Training Center (800).
New York:	Governors Island (3,451).
North Carolina:	Elizabeth City CG Support Center (674).
Virginia:	Yorktown CG Reserve Training Center (500).

Air Force—Stateside

Alabama: Gunter AFS (1,057); Maxwell AFB (1,924).

Alaska: Eielson AFB (2,600); Elmendorf AFB (9,500); King Salmon Airport (350); Shemya AFB (700).

Arizona: Davis-Monthan AFB (5,600); Gila Bend AF Auxiliary Field (325); Luke AFB (6,000); Williams AFB (3,200).

Arkansas: Blytheville AFB (2,688); Little Rock AFB (6,293).

California: Beale AFB (4,000); Castle AFB (5,800); Edwards AFB (3,657); George AFB (5,169); Los Angeles AFS (1,300); March AFB (4,149); Mather AFB (4,900); McClellan AFB (3,500); Norton AFB (7,500); Sunnyvale AFS (780); Travis AFB (13,400); Vandenberg AFB (4,741).

Colorado: Buckley Ang Base (400); Lowry AFB (8,132); Peterson AFB (3,445); U.S. Air Force Academy (2,550).

Delaware: Dover AFB (5,100).

District of Columbia: Bolling AFB (1,259).

Florida: Eglin AFB (includes Hurlbert Field) (13,000); Homestead AFB (5,352); MacDill AFB (6,200); Patrick AFB (3,400); Tyndall AFB (4,300).

Georgia: Moody AFB (2,900); Robins AFB (3,900).

Hawaii: Hickam AFB (5,100); Wheeler AFB (550).

Idaho: Mountain Home AFB (4,205).

Illinois: Chanute AFB (2,500); Scott AFB (6,322).

Indiana: Grissom AB (3,500).

Kansas: McConnell AFB (4,056).

Louisiana: Barksdale AFB (6,300); England AFB (3,000).

Maine: Loring AFB (3,400).

Maryland: Andrews AFB (6,600).

Massachusetts: Hanscom AFB (1,900).

Michigan: K. I. Sawyer AFB (4,000); Wurtsmith AFB (3,300).

Mississippi: Columbus AFB (2,971); Keesler AFB (6,500).

Missouri: Whiteman AFB (3,275).

Montana: Malmstrom AFB (5,200).

Nebraska: Offutt AFB (11,800).

Nevada: Nellis AFB (11,200).

New Hampshire: Pease AFB (3,100).

New Jersey: McGuire AFB (5,236).

New Mexico: Cannon AFB (4,000); Holloman AFB (5,600); Kirtland AFB (5,000).

New York: Griffiss AFB (4,000); Hancock Field (900); Plattsburgh AFB (4,200).

North Carolina: Pope AFB (3,962); Seymour Johnson AFB (5,000).

North Dakota: Grand Forks AFB (5,150); Minot AFB (5,500).

Ohio: Wright-Patterson AFB (7,900).

Oklahoma: Altus AFB (3,300); Tinker AFB (5,800); Vance AFB (1,121).

South Carolina: Charleston AFB (4,390); Myrtle Beach AFB (3,100); Shaw AFB (6,000).

South Dakota: Ellsworth AFB (5,885).
Texas: Bergstrom AFB (4,808); Brooks AFB (1,364); Carswell AFB (4,800); Dyess AFB (4,850); Goodfellow AFB (2,200); Kelly AFB (4,000); Lackland AFB (21,408); Laughlin AFB (2,500); Randolph AFB (5,532); Reese AFB (2,694); Sheppard AFB (8,138).
Utah: Hill AFB (5,500).
Virginia: Langley AFB (9,660).
Washington: Fairchild AFB (3,970); McChord AFB (6,250).
Wyoming: F. E. Warren AFB (3,710).

Air Force—Overseas

Australia
Azores
Belgium
Crete
Germany
Greece
Greenland
Guam
Iceland

Italy
Japan
Korea
Okinawa
Panama
Philippines
Spain
Turkey
United Kingdom

8. How To Enlist And Get What You Want

A person considering military service should be prepared to ask a lot of questions and expect to have them answered satisfactorily. For example:

How can I get the job I want?

Is it true that military recruiters will tell you *anything* to get your 'John Henry' on the enlistment contract?

What is my chance of being sent to the base or post where I want to go?

Can I qualify for an enlistment bonus?

Is the military's entrance examination tough?

I heard a lot of people fail the physical exam. Is that true?

Joining the service can be a frightening experience. Most young people arrive at the recruiter's office totally unprepared. Not only are they ignorant of who a recruiter is and what he does, but, more importantly, they do not know what questions to ask. The unfortunate result is that many enter the military with a job they really don't want. And after basic training, they are headed for a permanent military post thousands of miles from where they really would like to go.

This need not happen to you. And it won't—because this book will arm you with all the information you need to make your interview with the recruiter and subsequent processing a success, for you and the military. There's nothing a recruiter likes better than to sit down with a young person who knows what questions to ask and which of the many different enlistment options interests him or her. It makes the recruiter's job easier and enables him to focus on your needs and desires.

A wise shopper always checks out the quality of the merchandise and the reputation of the seller *before* he walks in the door. This chapter will help you become that wise and intelligent shopper, one who knows, before he ever enters the door of the recruiting office, such primary information as: what are the minimum qualifications for military service, the role of the recruiter, the importance of the service entrance exam, and how to ask for and get the enlistment options of his choice.

We'll be discussing the enlistment process. If you are interested in becoming an officer, the following chapter will help. It gives you much of the same information as this section does, but tailors it for interested officer candidates. Still, I recommend you read this as well because the information here will further assist you in understanding the selection process for military duty.

MINIMUM QUALIFICATIONS NEEDED

Before going any further, let's make sure you meet the *minimum* eligibility requirements for enlisted military service. To join any one of the five services, you must meet these requirements:

Age. Minimum age is 17. However, 17-year-olds will need permission of a parent or legal guardian. Maximum age varies by service, ranging from 28 to 35 years of age.

Citizenship. U.S. citizen or an immigrant alien lawfully admitted to the U.S. for permanent residence.

Physical. Must pass a physical exam given by the services. Ninety percent of the persons who take the services' physical pass it with flying colors. However, failure to meet physical standards is the single most frequent reason applicants are disqualified.

The services often disqualify a person for medical problems that are seemingly of a minor nature. Being overweight is the killer for many young persons. Other defects that can cause you to fail the physical exam are flat feet, peptic ulcers, extremely poor eyesight, hearing deficiencies, muscular or skeletal deficiencies, undescended testicles, ingrown toenails, and a host of other problems.

Many of these problems can be corrected. But, except for the Marines, the services will reject you based on the physical defect. If you have the problem corrected by a civilian doctor at your own expense, you may then reapply for enlistment. The Marines will take in persons with what are classified as "slight physical defects" and have them corrected, after enlistment, by Marine physicians.

Discuss with the recruiter any medical problems you have that might cause you to be disqualified for enlistment. It is possible that if you have been successfully treated for an ailment that might otherwise be disqualifying, you will need a statement from your doctor attesting that the deficiency has been corrected or will not cause a problem while you are in the service.

Education. For males, high school is desirable; for females, it's mandatory. GED (General Education Development) test certification is acceptable. However, even though the service may allow male applicants to enlist, they often reserve the best jobs for people with at least a high school diploma or the equivalent.

Also, the services may require non-high school graduates, or persons with only the equivalency, to score higher on the Armed Forces Qualification Test (AFQT), the services' entrance exam. For example, as of the date this book was written, the Air Force's minimum acceptable score on the AFQT was 21 for high school graduates, but persons with a GED diploma or other high school equivalency were required to make a 50 on the test, and non-high school graduates had to pass the exam with a score of 65 or better.

The best advice I can give you is that if you want to be a credit to yourself and to the service, *finish school*! Don't quit to join the military. Hang in there until graduation. You'll be a better person and better equipped to handle problems and pressures that will confront you. And the services can place you in a more desirable job position to take advantage of all your talents and abilities.

Moral. Almost everyone qualifies under the service's moral standards. However, if you admit to homosexual acts or if you have ever been arrested for moral offenses (prostitution, etc.), it may be difficult for you to qualify.

Involvement with Law Enforcement Authorities. This means trouble with the law. If you have ever been convicted or even arrested for any offense, no matter how small, you must inform the recruiter and provide information about the offense.

Not every violation of law will cause the service to reject you. The services will usually choose to overlook minor offenses such as traffic violations and misdemeanors such as disturbances of the peace. Even an isolated case of marijuana possession might be excused.

However, a *pattern* of law violations or an offense which involves moral turpitude or demonstrates violent or otherwise severe, socially unacceptable behavior may prevent your enlistment. The recruiter can give you more specifics.

It would be unwise for you to conceal from the recruiter any information about your involvement with the law. The recruiter will check out what you told him, and even if you manage to enlist and go on active duty after concealing this information, you could be discharged later.

Armed Forces Qualification Test (AFQT)

This is the test that many people believe—erroneously—is an intelligence test. You will have to take this exam, which is a part of the overall ASVAB test (Armed Services Vocational Aptitude Battery) and achieve a minimum acceptable score. Each service has a different standard, and the lowest score they will accept is a factor that changes frequently, depending on recruiting needs of the service. If, for instance, the Army is having difficulty in meeting its recruiting goals, the AFQT score minimum may be lowered to allow more people to qualify. If, however, things are going great on the recruiting front, the Army may increase the minimum score required of an applicant.

As of mid-1982, the minimum score on the AFQT an applicant must achieve to qualify for enlistment was as shown below:

Army:	High school graduate	16
	Non-high school graduate	50
	Women	50
Air Force:	Men and women: high school graduates	21
	Men: non-high school graduates	65
Navy:	Men and women: high school graduates	31
	Men: non-high school graduates	65

Marines:	Men: high school graduates	31
	Non-high school graduate—combined score of 100 on the math and word-knowledge portions of the ASVAB test, discussed later in this chapter.	
	Women	50
Coast Guard:	The Coast Guard does not use the AFQT as the basis for entrance. It has its own tests. However, if an applicant has already been administered the test by another branch of service, the Coast Guard will accept the results. In this case, the minimum acceptable scores for enlistment are:	
	Men and women: high school graduates	31
	Non-high school graduate	44

THE ENLISTMENT PROCESS

You've studied carefully the minimum eligibility requirements and you believe you have what it takes to be a U.S. serviceman or -woman. Not only that, but you have decided that service life is for you. Great. Now it's time to take the necessary steps for enlistment.

Enlisting is easy. If all you want is to join the service regardless of such considerations as what job you get, for how many years you must commit yourself, and where they'll send you, the enlistment process will be simple. Simply pass the ASVAB entrance exam and accept whatever the recruiter offers you. But being a manual laborer in uniform in the remote hinterlands of Equatorial Guinea probably doesn't appeal to you. (That's why you're reading this book, right?)

So how does the enlistment process work? There are essentially three steps you must take to become a uniformed member of the U.S. Armed Forces. First, you must take the Armed Services Vocational Aptitude Battery test (ASVAB); second, you have to talk with a military recruiter and begin the administrative paperwork; and, finally, you'll have to pay a visit to the Armed Forces Examining and Entrance Station (AFEES). Each of these steps is of utmost importance to your future in the military. We will consider each step in some detail.

The ASVAB

The first step toward enlistment—and probably the most crucial—is taking the Armed Services Vocational Aptitude Battery test (ASVAB). I can't overemphasize the importance of the ASVAB. You can complete the exam in just a couple of hours, but the results will stay with you your entire service career.

The ASVAB is composed of twelve different aptitude tests. It is not designed to determine how smart you are; it is *not* an intelligence test. It does give the services an idea of your general abilities and aptitudes. The ASVAB does this by measuring your aptitude in the areas of general information, numerical operations, attention to detail, word knowledge, electronic information, arithmetic reasoning, space perception, mathematics knowledge, mechanical comprehension, general science, shop information, and automotive information.

All of the services (except the Coast Guard) use the ASVAB to determine if you are service material and to decide in which career fields you might be eligible. The ASVAB is often given to high school students—juniors and seniors—at their schools or at other convenient locations. If you take it as a junior and aren't satisfied with your scores, you can retake it the following year. To take the test, ask your school counselor or principal or a military recruiter. Any military recruiter can administer the ASVAB test and the results will be honored by any of the services.

How the Services Use the ASVAB

The ASVAB takes only 2½ hours to complete, but it provides recruiters a huge amount of information. After you complete the exam, the testing officials will grade your responses and combine your scores on the 12 different "mini-tests" into several major areas:

- Verbal
- Math
- Perceptual speed
- Mechanical
- Trade technical
- Academic ability

How you score in each of these major areas determines the career fields and job specialties in the service for which you will be eligible. It's not difficult to understand why this is so. If, for instance, you score extremely low in verbal (word) skills, the services would be reluctant to assign you to an administrative job where verbal skills are essential to effective job performance. Likewise, if you score low in math, it's doubtful the service will take a chance on making you an accounting and finance specialist.

But let's say you score well in mechanical. You would then be a natural candidate, the service might conclude, for a job as an aircraft or automotive mechanic. And if your test results show that you are superb in academic ability, this might indicate your potential to tackle a complex and arduous curriculum at a service technical school.

Your scores on the ASVAB are given by percentile. In other words, you'll be given a score on each test area that tells you where you stand relative to everyone else in the nation who took the same test. So if you score 75 percentile, it means you did better on that part of the test than did 74 percent of the persons who took the test. On the other hand, it reflects that 25 percent of the test-takers did better than you.

Each of the services has a manual or book which lists the various occupations or job areas and gives the minimum score a recruit needs on the ASVAB to qualify. For a job as a heavy-vehicle repairperson, the Army may require you to score at least 40 in the mechanical area. To be a personnel specialist, the Air Force may desire a 50 in the verbal area.

The AFQT

In addition to using the ASVAB to determine your eligibility for a specific career field, the ASVAB results are used in an even more basic way—to test your aptitude for military service. Two of the individual ASVAB tests are combined to give you a composite score referred to as your Armed Forces Qualification Test (AFQT) score. This was discussed earlier, but it is so important that I want to touch on it again.

You *must* make the acceptable minimum score on the AFQT to be eligible to serve in the armed forces. As previously discussed, each service has its own standard of acceptability.

The AFQT is often called the mental exam. So if you hear someone say that a guy or gal has "flunked" the service mental exam, that person is referring to the AFQT. The services have spent millions of dollars to design the ASVAB and its subcomponent, the AFQT. Studies have shown that the test scores are reliable. Although they do not adequately reflect intelligence, they do have the capability of predicting a person's success or failure both in the service itself and in a specific occupation or career area.

Preparing for the ASVAB

You can't exactly study for an aptitude test since it doesn't test your knowledge of a specific body of information. Nevertheless, you will perform better on the test if you understand the types of questions it contains.

If you want to prepare for the ASVAB by becoming familiar with the questions, your best bet is to obtain, *Practice for Army Placement Tests* (Arco Publishing, 1982). This book explains the ASVAB at length and has a number of sample questions covering the various areas of the test. I highly recommend you get this book and work with it for at least several weeks prior to taking the ASVAB.

Remember that the ASVAB can be your ticket to a bright, new future. Prepare for the test, get a good night's sleep the night before you take the test, and do your best in answering the questions. Your understanding of the test's importance and your mental preparation will put you ahead of other applicants, and possibly get you that great job and advanced service school you want so much.

Your Obligation.   Your taking the ASVAB does not obligate you in any way to the service. It doesn't cost you a cent to take it. Even if you decide that the service is not for you, the ASVAB will be a valuable tool to help you personally decide on your future. This is because the ASVAB will give you a clear picture of your own personal strengths and weaknesses. It can guide you toward the civilian career or occupation for which you are best suited. The ASVAB would be a bargain even if the services charged for it. Thankfully, they don't.

Getting the Results.   Depending on who administers the ASVAB, the test results may be available to your recruiter within a few days, or you may end up on pins and needles for as long as 30 days, awaiting the score.

YOUR MILITARY RECRUITER

With the ASVAB taken and your scores in hand, it's time to talk with the recruiter from the service of your choice. Young people often grow apprehensive and nervous when the word *recruiter* is echoed aloud. Military recruiters don't have the best of reputations in our society. They are often pictured as fast-talking con artists who will tell a young person positively anything to get him or her to sign on the dotted line. Actually, this is an unfair characterization of the military recruiter. Like any other stereotype, there are only a few recruiters, out of the more than 10,000 nationwide, who do, perhaps, deserve this unbecoming reputation.

Several years ago, an Army scandal resulted in the firing of several hundred of that service's military recruiters. The overzealous Army recruiters, it was alleged, falsified documents of non-high school graduates to make it appear that they had high school diplomas. Some recruiters also fraudulently gave new recruits higher scores on the AFQT than they legitimately had earned. This scandal resulted in a general housecleaning by the Army and by all the services. The "bad apple" recruiters were fired and systems were set up to insure that only honest and forthright procedures are used.

Today, military recruiters can be expected to "tell it like it is" about your prospects in the service and about military life in general. You can expect your recruiter to be frank and honest. Naturally, he will be positive about his own branch of service and will color his remarks accordingly. It's his job to do so. But, then, you didn't really expect the Navy recruiter (or the Air Force recruiter, etc.) to say negative things about the Navy, did you? After all, would you expect a Ford or Chevrolet salesperson to make derogatory remarks about their own products?

The military recruiter is above all a salesperson—and usually a darned good one at that! He has been selected for recruiting duty only after years of faithful service during which he proved his loyalty and demonstrated outstanding performance. The services generally assign only their best non-commissioned officers as recruiters. They are put through a rigorous and demanding training program that hones and sharpens their speaking ability and their sales skills.

The Role of the Recruiter

The recruiter's role is to advise you on your future in uniform. He keeps up with personnel policies, life-style changes, and assignment rules for his service, and he should be able to answer any questions you might have. The fact that recruiters successfully enlist hundreds of thousands of people (367,500 in 1980) gives you an indication of their skill in performing their job.

While he may not know all the intimate details about each and every occupational area and job and each and every unit and military station, he knows about as much as any one person can. What he doesn't know he will be able to research for you and ultimately answer.

The recruiter can administer the ASVAB test to you and he can counsel you on the results. He cannot guarantee you that there will be a job opening in the field in which you are most interested—as we'll later discuss, that's the job of the career guidance counselor at the AFEES Station (your next step in the enlistment process)—but the recruiter *can* tell you for what jobs you are qualified. He can advise you about the schooling the service will provide for you for the job, and he can explain the many enlistment options his service offers.

How to Work with the Recruiters

The best way to get what you want when you join the service is to work closely with the recruiter. Show him that you have done your homework and that you already know something about a few of your options. Don't be cocky or a "know-it-all," but do try to demonstrate to the recruiter that you are seriously, and carefully, considering military service. Reading this book is a splendid way to prepare, and especially to narrow down the service of your choice. Another must is to drop in at the recruiting station and pick up all the free brochures and pamphlets they have to offer. Then, if you have questions about what you're reading, phone and ask a recruiter or an assistant at his office.

When you are convinced you're ready to actually talk to the recruiter on a serious level, call and make an appointment to see him at his office. You can arrange to meet him on "neutral ground"—at your home or at school—but this would be inconvenient and impractical because the recruiter has all his manuals, pay charts, and other reference material at his office and might not be able to answer all your questions.

Prior to your formal visit, make a written list of all the questions you want to ask the recruiter and the topics you want to discuss. When you arrive at the recruiter's office for your interview, look sharp and act with maturity. Hair that needs shampooing, clothes that need washing and ironing, and a posture that cries out "I don't care," is not the way to get the recruiter on your side.

For those who protest that the recruiter need not be on your side, that he is *obligated* to enlist you, like it or not, all I can say is that you need a lesson in human behavior. While it is true that, legally, the recruiter must take your application and process it, how he handles it and the degree of zeal and enthusiasm he has for you can be significant.

With all the diverse enlistment options available today, enlisting in the armed forces can be a confusing and frustrating experience. The recruiter is trained to provide the facts you need to know and to answer your questions about the military and the various enlistment options. If you alienate him and show him a lack of respect by displaying a negative or apathetic attitude, he'll likely conclude that you are unsuited for the service. Sure, he'll give you the information you demand and take your application material, but he won't go out of his way to help you.

The smart young person actively seeks the help of the recruiter and demonstrates an aptitude and desire for service. He has the kind of attitude and physical demeanor that is becoming to a future member of the U.S. military. When the recruiter recognizes this in a young person, you can expect him to knock himself out to help that individual get what he or she deserves from the service.

The Incompetent Recruiter

Not all recruiters are equal in ability and personality. Although the services try to select only the most outstanding people for this duty, every once in a while a dud slips through. Naturally, an incompetent recruiter—one who either doesn't do the job the way it should be done or else has an irritating personality—hurts the image of the service he represents. Incompetent and uncaring recruiters are few in number and, when found out, the services are quick to relieve them of their duties.

What do you do if you visit the recruiter's office and feel he isn't giving you the help you need—that he's incompetent? I would recommend you do one or more of the following three things: report his behavior to his superior; ask to see another recruiter in the same office (if one is available); or go to another recruiting station.

The third alternative is preferred, but if you feel it necessary to seek out another recruiter to get the assistance you are due, you should report the incompetent or impolite recruiter to his superior. Don't just forget the incident; instead, consider that if he gave you the bum's rush, he's probably done the same to others. Do them and the service a favor and lodge a complaint to his boss or someone higher in authority. Remember that in the military, *everyone* has a higher authority somewhere up the ladder, including recruiters.

The Recruiter Next Door

If you feel you're not getting all the facts from one recruiter, feel free to visit another station and see another recruiter. You're under no obligation to work with the recruiter nearest home. There are thousands of recruiting stations across the U.S; the Army alone has 2,000. The Army also has a grand total of 6,000 recruiters, the vast majority of whom are thorough, caring professionals.

Across the city or in the town next door is another recruiting station and another group of experienced recruiters eager and willing to see that you get every option for which you qualify and concerned that you enter active duty as a proud and happy member of their service.

ENLISTMENT OPTIONS

The services offer a number of enlistment options. These are written promises or guarantees in which the service certifies that you will get what you want in the way of the career field, choice of training, and duty location. Enlistment options might also let you use the "buddy plan" in which you and a friend enlist together and stay together through boot camp.

One option is in regard to your term of enlistment. You can sign up for two, three, four, or six years, depending on the service and the job you want. Another option allows you to sign up now but delay going on active duty.

Two options of great importance to your pocketbook are the cash bonus plan and a program in which you are given advanced, preferential promotions for your civilian job experience, or formal college education you have acquired.

These options are not guaranteed to you by word alone. Both you and the recruiter, representing the military, must sign a binding contract. This contract is so vitally important that you should read it with utmost care and attention. Take a copy of it home if need be and let your parents or an adult whom you respect look over it. Know what you are signing.

Following are descriptions of some of the more important options you may decide on if you are eligible.

Delayed Entry Program (DEP). This option is attractive for many people because it permits you to sign up now for enlistment, getting the job of your choice, and go on active duty later—up to 365 days later in some cases.

Why would you decide to delay entering the service? This option is really a personal one. Maybe you wish to give yourself a "breather" for a few months after completing high school. Or perhaps you have some unfinished business at home to take care of or a civilian job commitment to keep.

There's also the matter of the job field you wish to enter. If the job you want is not available at the time you first talk to the recruiting personnel, it is possible to use the DEP program to reserve the job in the future.

Whatever the reason you wish to delay going on active duty, the Delayed Entry Program can help by postponing your entry date.

Enlistment Bonuses.   One of the more profitable options is the offer of a cash bonus for enlisting in a specific hard-to-fill career field job. Both the Army and Navy offer these bonuses, which are paid to you after you complete training.

These bonuses can be sizeable. At press time, the Army was doling out up to $5,000 in cash for enlistment in combat fields like infantry and armor and in the support areas such as intelligence, languages, and electronics. The Navy's bonus was limited to $2,000, but you could get it for entry into any one of several different fields.

However, there is a catch to the enlistment bonuses. In most cases, you will have to agree to a term of military service that is more than the minimum. The Army has two-, three-, and four-year enlistments, but doesn't offer bonuses on two- and three-year enlistees. The Navy will ask you to agree to six full years to be eligible for their bonus.

Choice of Job.   All of the services have an option that allows you to choose the job you want *before* enlisting. If there is an opening in the field and you are qualified by your score on the ASVAB, the job is yours. The service *guarantees* it and it is written into your enlistment contract.

The services do try their best to fit you into the job of your choice. By advance planning with computers, they know in what job areas they will be needing people in the foreseeable future. This permits them the flexibility to guarantee you a job, and to keep their promise.

All the services except the Air Force guarantee *all* of their jobs, so when you report for active duty, you know exactly what job you'll have after training. Currently, the Air Force can guarantee you a job in 95 percent of their specialties in the mechanical area, 85 percent of those in the administrative fields, and 80 percent in the electronics occupations. In the general field, which includes a great variety of skills such as supply, security police, and recreational specialists, 30 percent of the jobs are guaranteed.

However, before you jump with joy believing it a cinch that you'll be guaranteed a specific job, you should bear one key point in mind: the job is guaranteed only if it is available! Now, this sounds like double-talk, so let me explain. To enlist in the service, you'll be required to visit an Armed Forces Examination and Entrance Station (AFEES). There you will formally and officially be advised what specific jobs are available and if you are eligible. If the job you want is available, you can be *guaranteed* the job. You simply tell the AFEES guidance counselor that you will enlist for that job and it's yours!*

---

*We'll talk more about the role of the AFEES guidance counselor later in this chapter, on page 98.

On the other hand, if it's not available—i.e., if the service doesn't need people in that particular job at that time—you will be advised accordingly and offered another for which you are eligible. In effect, then, you can be guaranteed a specific job before enlistment, as long as the service has a current need.

Field of Choice. If you wish to join the Air Force and the specific job you want is not available, you might opt for one of four broad career fields instead: mechanical, administrative, general, and electronics.

Under this program, the Air Force guidance counselor at AFEES will brief you about the types of jobs that the field encompasses. He will tell you, for example, that the mechanical field includes a multitude of different jobs. By enlisting in the mechanical field, you would be guaranteed one of these jobs. You would not know which one—whether in the areas of missile, aircraft, or automotive skills, for instance—but at least you would have a job within the desired overall area.

Later, during boot camp, you will have an opportunity to ask for a *specific* job within, say, the mechanical field, which you may get. However, there is no guarantee.

Advanced Rank Option. This option goes by a different name in each service. But whatever title the service gives, the Advanced Rank Option is a plan that allows a person to enter military service with more stripes on his arm and more money in his paycheck.

One of the ways you can do this is to receive advanced rank for post-high school education. If you have completed one or more years of college, you can start at a higher rank and with more pay than someone without any college credits. Usually you will be given E-3 pay grade, which will place you two full steps above your contemporaries.

Another way to get advanced rank is to volunteer for a career field that is so technical or so hard to fill that few people qualify for it. The Navy, in particular, has several fields that to start with will net you advanced rank. One is the nuclear field; another is the advanced electronics field. There's also advanced rank for boiler technicians, hospital corpspeople, and engineers.

All of these fields usually have one thing in common: they require your completion of lengthy training schools and a long period of enlistment, typically six years.

Civilian Experience Option. This is another program that gets you off to a fast start in the military. The Direct Procurement Enlistment Program (DPEP) is what the Navy calls its program, but the Army has a similar program by another name.

Here's how it works: if you have civilian training or work experience that the military needs, you may be eligible to enlist directly in a higher rank. How high a rank depends on your level of civilian skills and training. A look at the Navy's program will give you an idea of how attractive this option can be if you can meet the required criteria.

To qualify for the Navy DPEP, you must have attended a vocational/technical school, or completed some on-the-job training, or participated in certain industrial apprenticeship programs. And you must have had a certain amount of work experience putting those skills to use in a civilian job.

The program is especially designed for men and women who achieved their training in civilian life. The Navy knows that it takes hard work to get through vocational school—they also know that experience is the best teacher—and believe that hard work and experience should be recognized and put to good use, which is the reasoning behind this special program.

The program is open in over 50 Navy job areas, and it allows for enlistment as a petty officer at any of several levels, depending on your age and your training, work, and supervisory experience. The length of your formal vocational or technical school education counts for up to one-half the work experience requirement. If you meet these requirements and can submit evidence of qualified work experience that ended within the past year, check the chart entitled "Civilian Experience Option—Navy" (Figure 8-1, below). It summarizes the requirements and the petty officer ratings under which you can join the Navy if you qualify for the DPEP.

Minimum Age (Max. age is 32)	Vocational Training or Equivalent (Counts as ½ Required Work Experience)	Required Years of Work Experience	Rating & Pay Grade
20	1 yr. or 1,000 hrs.	2 yrs.	Petty Officer 3d Class (E-4)
23	2 yrs. or 2,000 hrs.	4 yrs. including 6 mos. supervisory	Petty Officer 2d Class (E-5)
26	3 yrs. or 3,000 hrs.	6 yrs. including 1 yr. supervisory	Petty Officer 1st Class (E-6)
28	4 yrs. or 4,000 hrs.	8 yrs. including 1½ yrs. supervisory	Chief Petty Officer (E-7)

Civilian Experience Option—Navy

Figure 8-1.

Once you've joined the Navy through this program, you can be sure that your acquired vocational skills will be used to good advantage during your four-year enlistment because the purpose of the DPEP is to help skilled workers use their talents to become better craftsmen.

How valuable is this program? Well, just consider the situation of an individual with three years of vocational training in a civilian skill and four and one-half years of work experience. His starting military pay would be about $1,300 a month, plus benefits. He would have all of the added status and prestige of higher rank without one day of military service experience.

Regrettably, the Air Force and Marines do not offer this option, but they do take your civilian skills and knowledge into account in determining your suitability for a specific military job. If you opt to join one of these branches, at least your civilian training will be recognized and used.

Station-of-choice Option. This option can be rewarding in that it assures you of training in a specialty and then a follow-up assignment to any military post in the U.S. Also, you're guaranteed of being allowed to stay at least one year at the selected location.

Some enlistees treasure this option because it permits them to stay close to home (or, perhaps, travel far away from home!) or to be assigned to a post with exceptional facilities. Some persons use the option to be assigned to a site near a civilian college or university they wish to attend in their off-duty time.

Airborne Option. Want to jump out of airplanes? Your Army recruiter can fix you up. Provided you are physically fit—this is one tough course—you could be sent directly to parachute school after boot camp.

Band Option. For people who have musical talent and band skills and who want a job in an Army band, this is the way to do it. Don't get the idea that anyone who toots a horn or bangs on a drum can be a military band member. This is an elite bunch of musicians. If you wish to join them, you'll be auditioned and must survive a highly competitive screening process. But if you have the necessary professional skills and this option appeals to you, check it out.

Unit-of-choice Option. Again, this program goes by different names, but works essentially the same in the services that offer it. It is designed to let you choose the unit to which you want to be first assigned after initial training.

If you know of a specific unit—combat, support, or medical—of which you want to be a part, this option can guarantee your assignment to that unit. As with most other options, you will have to agree to serve more than the minimum number of years on your enlistment.

Iron-clad Guarantee. All of these options sound good. Who doesn't want such plums as earning a hefty enlistment bonus, getting the job, station and unit of choice, and starting out at an advanced rank? But, you might ask, can I really trust the recruiter? What happens if the service welches on its promise?

Occasionally, in years past, this was a problem. A young man promised an electronics job at Fort Knox, Kentucky, might have ended up as a cook in Jumblott, Wyoming! That is no longer the case. As I stated earlier, if you are eligible and apply for one or more of these option programs, you will be presented a detailed contract guaranteeing you'll get what you're promised. Courts have held that the services must comply with this contract, and they do. If you don't get what was promised you, you can ask to be released from your service commitment, and you will be. That's an iron-clad guarantee.

Enlisting

If what you have found out from the recruiter, from this book and other sources has made you decide to be a part of your nation's defense forces, you'll need to take certain actions to enlist. The first, of course, is to let the recruiter know of your decision and to arrange a visit to his office.

On this visit bring with you the following documents to give to the recruiter:

- Birth certificate
- High school diploma or other certification that you have attended high school. GED documentation if you have completed the high school equivalency test.
- Social Security card
- Letter from your doctor if you have (or had) any special medical condition that the service's physicians may need information on to certify you as medically qualified.

The recruiter will review these documents and prepare the paperwork you will need to complete the next step in the enlistment process—the AFEES.

THE TIME HAS COME—AFEES

Everyone who enlists in the armed services must process through an Armed Forces Examination and Entrance Station (AFEES). There are 69 of these stations nationwide, each strategically located to serve a great number of personnel in a specific geographical area. The recruiter will arrange for you to be processed at the nearest AFEES station and, if necessary, he will provide transportation and even meals for overnight lodging.

The AFEES are manned by personnel from all of the services. They can be busy places. The Chicago station processes about 70,000 people each year. Of those, about 90 percent are found qualified.

What does AFEES do to aid your enlistment? Their mission encompasses several tasks. We can best examine what this mission is by taking a look at what awaits you on a typical day at the AFEES.

Your day at the AFEES starts early in the morning. About 7 A.M. you will be briefed on what to expect and you'll have an opportunity to ask questions about the various steps in your processing. Don't be afraid to ask any questions. After this briefing, you are ready to start your processing. This is divided into four general areas: mental, medical, personnel, and administrative.

The mental evaluation is the ASVAB test described earlier in this chapter. If you followed the procedure given in this book, you will have already taken this test and seen the results. Some enlistees, however, will not have taken the exam and so the AFEES administers it to those who need it.

Next stop is the medical examination. Medical doctors and trained technicians will perform this examination, which may be the most thorough physical check you will ever have had. Any pertinent medical documents or letters from your doctor that you have not already given to your recruiter should be turned in at this time. This will help the AFEES doctor in evaluating your physical condition. Women will be examined separately and in privacy, with a female escort present. The women undergo the same rigorous exam as do the men, with their individual sexual differences taken into account.

Your physical examination will take about two hours. After it is completed, you will have a brief conference with the doctor. If any medical problems have been discovered, he will go over these with you. Most of the time there won't be any and you'll proceed to the third step in the AFEES screening—the ultra-important personnel counseling.

The Guidance Counselor

Personnel counseling is accomplished in a one-on-one visit with the guidance counselor of the service branch in which you plan to enlist. This is the moment that you have been waiting for, the time when you are told if you can get the job, station, and training that you want.

The guidance counselor will discuss with you your specific enlistment options. He will then take your ASVAB scores, physical evaluation and other information—such as your recruiter's documents regarding your civilian training and experience—and feed this data into a small computer. This computer is called a

REQUEST terminal. It will analyze the data, compare it with his service's eligibility requirements, and immediately advise you on what you're qualified for and what is available. Hopefully, this determination of your eligibility for the career field and other options you want will not differ from what you were told by your recruiter. However, in the final analysis, the guidance counselor is the authority. He is specially trained for his job and has the computer's knowledge to back him up.

The computer terminal used by the guidance counselor is actually a remote instrument. Inputs to the terminal come direct from the service's personnel headquarters. For instance, the Air Force's Military Personnel Center at Randolph Air Force Base, Texas, programs the Air Force's REQUEST terminals at the AFEES station. It is important to understand how this is done.

As Air Force (Army, Navy, or Marine) needs change, the computer is reprogrammed. This insures that only so many aircraft maintenance specialists, administrative personnel, carpentry technicians, etc., are enlisted. Also, the computer is programmed to add or delete bases that are open under the base-of-choice option and it is updated as to the current status of other enlistment options.

So when the guidance counselor requests current information, it is available on his REQUEST terminal. This has great impact on what you will get. If, for example, you asked for guaranteed assignment at Mather Air Force Base, California, as a heating and refrigeration specialist, and the computer says that no slots are available at that base, all your hopes and desires go out the window! If you want to be in Army Intelligence and the terminal says you need a 50 verbal score on the ASVAB—and your score was 40—sorry.

The REQUEST terminal spells out exactly what is available. If you are fortunate, it will list the very option that you want. If it does, you're in the chips! Give the guidance counselor the "go ahead" and you're on your way to joining your comrades in uniform. He confirms a reservation on the computer terminal and all that's left to do is sign the enlistment contract.

But what if it doesn't? What if the terminal brings forth the depressing news that the job and other options you want most are not available? In that case, the guidance counselor will offer suggestions that both fit your qualifications and the needs of the service. But before you agree and sign the contract, think it over. The news that the job you had your heart set on is not available can be a crushing disappointment. But don't make matters worse by jumping at the chance to take just any alternative the guidance counselor suggests. You are under no obligation to do so, so don't feel pressured.

If you need time to think things over, you can leave the AFEES station and postpone a decision until you have fully investigated the job and option offered you. In the course of this investigation you might wish to again talk with the recruiter and obtain his advice. The important thing is that you know what you're getting into *before* you commit yourself.

However, there is a danger in delaying too long. As I said, the AFEES computers are regularly updated to reflect current needs. This means that the longer you wait, the more likely it is that the computer's information will be revised. You may find, to your dismay, that even the alternative option suggestion by the AFEES guidance counselor is removed from availability. This is a chance you are taking if you wait.

However, another result may also occur. It is conceivable—though not probable—that your first choice of job and options may become available during the interim. Thus, you may find, to your delight and surprise, that you can enlist and get what you originally wanted and asked for on your first visit to the AFEES station after all. However, don't count on this happening, and be prepared to accept a reasonable alternative if you still wish to enlist.

It May be Greener on the Other Side

If the service that is your first choice can't offer you the enlistment options that you want, you should feel free to check with the guidance counselor of the other services. Your successful completion of the AFEES processing makes you eligible for enlistment in any branch of service, depending on your having attained the appropriate ASVAB and AFQT scores required by a particular branch.

Unless wearing green, blue, white, or tan is of overwhelming importance to you, it may pay to check out what the other services have to offer. You may find that the Navy has just the job or option that the Marines say is unavailable, or vice versa.

DEAL ME IN

Nowadays, most people are pleased at the alternatives offered them by the AFEES guidance counselor. Unlike the old days, when the service decided for you, today a person usually has a number of options. Of course, the higher your scores on the ASVAB, the more likely you will get what you want. But service veterans will tell you that even a career field that at first sounds unpleasant often turns out to be rewarding and worthwhile.

Still, you may decide that what the service has to offer is unacceptable in terms of your personal goals and aspirations. In that case, you haven't lost a thing in investigating your options, and, through the ASVAB, you may have a better feel for what jobs or training you may productively pursue as a civilian.

On the other hand, if the service is for you and you tell the guidance counselor, "Deal me in," the challenge of boot camp awaits you.

9. Boot Camp

Everyone—I mean *everyone*—who has ever been in the military can tell you fascinating tales about their experiences at boot camp. Some people could regale you for hours with stories of bizarre and strange happenings at places like Fort Polk, Lackland, and Parris Island, and everything they say is probably true!

Hairless and Bewildered . . . A Boot Camp Story

Not too long ago, the Commandant of the U.S. Marine Corps, General Robert H. Barrow, addressed the Pennsylvania House of Representatives. He told the following humorous story, which he claimed was true.

All recruits in the Marine Corps who go to Parris Island, South Carolina, come initially to Charleston by air. Then they are put aboard chartered buses if there is a large contingent, or if only a few come in, they may ride the regular bus from Charleston to Savannah, which would come into Parris Island and let off those few. It is always at night, usually about 1 o'clock in the morning.

Back about 1973, when I was commanding general down there, the regular Charleston-to-Savannah bus run had aboard about 12 incoming recruits who were on their way to Paris Island for boot camp. The bus pulled up to the recruit receiving barracks, where a drill instructor stuck his head in the door and, in that kind of commanding voice they all have, said, "ALL RIGHT, OFF THE BUS!"

The 12 recruits got off the bus and so did a young, 16-year-old lad on his way from Charleston to Savannah to visit his grandmother.

Three days later, had you been at Parris Island, you would have seen this individual who looked like a recruit. His hair was gone, he had a bewildered look about him. But he was riding around in a Marine Corps sedan, being given a cook's tour of the place before he was very carefully delivered to his grandmother's house in Savannah.

A UNIQUE EXPERIENCE

Boot camp is definitely an unusual and unique experience. It will be your first acquaintance with real military life—and what an acquaintance! From the moment you arrive—by bus, air, rail, taxi, or whatever—things will be popping all over. Your head begins to reel as you stand facing your new training instructor. He barks strange new commands at you and the other assembled recruits and carries on like he's Hitler and Napoleon all wrapped into one. You ask yourself, "Is this real? Am I really here?"

The first few days at boot camp, even the first week or two can be a shock. Just being told what to do in absolute and unquestionably harsh terms is a new experience for many. Sure, you've followed instructions before from parents, teachers, and maybe a superior in a retail store or fast-food restaurant in which you worked part-time. But it wasn't anything like this! The word *please* doesn't seem to be in your instructor's vocabulary. However, words like *dummy, ignorant, sloppy, slow, terrible*, and much, much worse seem to roll off his tongue like molasses.

Nothing you do seems to please him. You made your bunk bed tighter than a drum and, as you stood proudly by it while the instructor inspected, all you heard was a snarl and a comment that it could be better. Yes, things sure weren't like this back home! You question whether you can last one more week. *Maybe I should quit*, you reason. But you don't; you just wish the military nightmare would end.

After the first few weeks, things begin to brighten up. The tasks that took you hours to do the first few days—like "spitshining" your boots and arranging your locker—now take only a few minutes of your time. Even the instructor seems to have mellowed. He's still no "Mr. Nice Guy," but at least he doesn't stick his nose a quarter of an inch from yours while he hollers with all the strength of his powerful vocal chords.

Still, things are no picnic. Boot camp is a monotony of 5 A.M. wake-up calls and marching in formation as the sun heats your body and sweat pours off your forehead. Carrying that heavy pack around out in the field isn't one iota of fun. You can take it, though, and see it through to the end, you decide. It's not as tough as you first thought.

Amazingly, by graduation day an incredible transformation has taken place. By now, you've come to the conclusion that boot camp wasn't so bad after all. In fact, it's only a cut above Boy Scout camp! Everything seems to be going so smoothly. Why, your instructor doesn't even come around much. Instead, he has delegated a lot of his authority to you and your fellow recruits. He trusts you! He hasn't said a disparaging word for over a week, and yesterday he gave a little speech to everyone about how proud he is of you and what an outstanding bunch of soldiers you are!

You feel great about yourself. You're in excellent condition—the best of your life. You're mentally alert and feel you've successfully taken everything boot camp could throw at you, and you came up smelling like roses—a real winner! *The folks back home are going to be proud of me*, you decide, pride and spirit swelling up inside. You've accepted the challenge and have become a member of the best fighting force in the world!

THE LESSONS OF BOOT CAMP

Everyone experiences the excitement, rigors, and demands of boot camp in their own way and from their own unique frame of reference. But everyone who completes it successfully and graduates will tell you that it made them a better person. Even if you feel the inspections were "Mickey Mouse" and picayune, the food was mediocre, and you were picked on and harassed, you begin to understand that it was all for your own good, and for the good of your country.

After all the drills and lectures and the pains and push-ups, you'll know that discipline and responsibility, two key attributes learned in boot camp, are the cornerstone of an effective military force; and, most important, they are the key to success in civilian life, too.

They used to say that boot camp would make a man out of a boy. No one uses that phraseology anymore, and they shouldn't. Boot camp won't make you into a man—or a woman. Don't expect it to change your life or make you over. Boot camp will, however, bring out the best in you. You'll be surprised at your ability to rapidly learn new things and apply them and at the sense of pride and responsibility you will develop over just a short span of time.

Boot camp is worthwhile. America needs trained and disciplined men and women. You can bet that our nation's enemies have just as tough a boot camp for their armed forces personnel—tougher even than ours. In fact, the brutal and harsh conditions of military training in a nation like the Soviet Union, or in most other countries around the world, would seem intolerable to the average American military recruit. In comparison, our own boot camp programs are relatively mild and the surroundings plush. Yes, boot camp isn't your Sunday picnic, but it is necessary and, on graduation day, you fully realize how valuable the experience has been.

You also realize the value of the close friendships you have forged with the other guys and gals in your training group. You all came from different areas of the country—from New York, California, Texas, Florida, and Ohio—but you shared an experience together and are all part of the same team. Probably the friendships you made in boot camp will endure for many years to come.

Most servicepeople say they'd never go through boot camp again. But you'll never hear a serviceperson—or a veteran—say they're sorry they did it or that it was a waste of effort.

A BOOT CAMP PRIMER

The very thought of going through weeks of strenuous and exacting military training in boot camp frightens many people. It needn't frighten you, not if you know what to expect and prepare yourself for it, mentally and physically. To help you prepare, it is a good idea to examine what boot camp is and what it isn't.

What It Is

Boot camp goes by different names. In the Air Force, it's basic training; the Navy calls it recruit training; the Army, initial entry training; and the Marines . . . well, leave it to Marines to call it—what else?—just plain old boot camp.

Whatever title it is given, boot camp is where you learn the basics of military life. You'll march until you feel your feet will come off, you'll be hassled endlessly, and the old saying, "Hurry up and wait," will take on a new and intimate meaning to you.

Your hair will be the first thing to go. You won't have much time to comb and groom it anyway. And your civilian clothes? They'll be stored in safekeeping for you. When you're issued your uniforms, you'll feel good about it. *All these new, free clothes*, you'll think. But, then, the realization will set in that no longer are you an individual. Everyone is dressed alike. There's no room for individuality in boot camp.

Your training instructor will be a highly trained, experienced, and capable veteran. The job of training instructor is a difficult and visible one. If he is not competent and does not train his troops (e.g., recruits) to his superior's satisfaction by graduation day, he'll be in a lot of trouble.

You don't need to know very much about military life when you arrive at boot camp; your service's instructor will teach you everything you need to know—how to march, drill, shave, eat, wash, shoot, everything. You'll learn about service traditions, courtesies, rank, and orders. You'll know all there is to know about caring for your uniform and wearing it proudly. If you didn't learn them well before, you'll be given ample instruction on how to say "Yes, sir" and "No excuse, sir!"

To do well at boot camp you should strive to do your best to get along and relate with your peers. Your group or unit will be called a flight, a platoon, or a company. Its composition will vary, depending on the service. All the people in your unit are in the same boat. They are good Americans who want to succeed, and they want you to succeed. Be a friend and a helper to them and they'll befriend you. Act superior, cocky, aloof, or smart-alecky, and your life at boot camp will be miserable indeed.

Boot camp isn't for everyone; a few will be weeded out. For one reason or another, they won't be suitable for military service. Perhaps they are not amenable to discipline, refuse to practice good hygiene, or simply don't have the ability and intelligence to carry out instructions. A few people will crack under the pressure. Somehow, these people slipped through the recruiter's screening and the AFEES process.

The training instructor is trained to spot the persons early who don't have what it takes to be in the service. He will give such a person every opportunity to improve his performance. But if he can't—or won't—the instructor will recommend an honorable discharge. And it almost always is approved, although occasionally the commanding officer will give the individual a second chance.

In many cases, a person who is not progressing in training will be *recycled* or *set back*. In this instance, he will be put back with another unit a few weeks behind his own in training. This is good in that he will now have a new training instructor and a new group of peers to work with—a fresh start. If he then applies himself, he is home free and will go on to successfully graduate.

What It Isn't

First and foremost, boot camp is not a rose garden. Recruiters don't say too much about the tough life that awaits the recruit. After all, they don't wish to dwell on the negative. But if asked, they usually are frank about it.

Boot camp is not a place where you will be physically abused. Sure, your Marine DI (drill instructor) may make you give him 20 (push-ups) because you talked in formation, and your Navy company commander (the Navy's title for instructor) may scare the dickens out of you with his rough and threatening tone of voice. But you won't be touched physically or manhandled in any way.

Years ago, there were several scandals of maltreatment of recruits, and periodically a case or two still arises and is reported in the media. This is rare. Instructors and other personnel at boot camp are given firm instructions never to lay a hand on a recruit. If they do, their careers are over, and they could be court-martialed.

If you receive any kind of physical abuse in boot camp, go directly to your unit's commanding officer and report it. If this doesn't work, demand to see the Inspector General or even the camp, post, or base commander. You won't get into any trouble if your allegations are true, but your instructor will!

Preparing Yourself

Boot camp will be a lot easier and even be minimally enjoyable if you arrive there physically and mentally prepared. Because you'll end up marching over a hundred miles, doing calisthenics, running an hour or more a day, and be on the go from sunup to bedtime, it's best to show up for training in excellent physical condition. If not, at least be in reasonably good shape. Running a mile or two and doing 30 minutes or so of calisthenics daily should have you in fine mettle for boot camp.

It's also important to prepare yourself mentally. In doing this, there are several things you should do.

• Remember that boot camp will be demanding, but millions of other young men and women have gone before you, and they made it. You can, too.

• Keep in mind that attitude is 99 percent of the solution for an outstanding performance at boot camp. You've passed the service's medical screening and its AFQT test. They've stamped your records "Fit for Duty." Now, it's up to you. If you want it bad enough and are willing to express a "can do" attitude, you'll go through it with flying colors.

• Have a sense of proportion—and humor—about what befalls you in boot camp. At times, you'll feel the training instructor is singling you out unfairly. And you'll be right. He takes turns testing everyone, so your time *will* come. Often, at the end of the day, you'll be frayed around the edges, tired, and sore. And you'll come back to the barracks to find your bed torn apart by your instructor and a note telling you your town pass is revoked. In times like these, your best bet is to sigh, smile inside and just keep chugging along, doing your darndest to be the best soldier, airman, sailor, or marine possible.

Someday, after boot camp is over, you'll look back on it all and have a good laugh. "Wasn't that crazy when Sergeant Wilson gave Jones that demerit for having a cockroach in his footlocker?" you'll ask yourself. "And, how about Tim Ross, the guy who bunked next to me. Boy, he really could tell some jokes. Of course, he couldn't march—had two left feet—but he sure kept us all in stitches."

It is well to prepare yourself in advance for the trauma of boot camp by accepting the coming hardships as inevitable. Tell yourself that it is serious, and that you'll put forth your best effort, but you won't take it so seriously that things will get out of proportion. Above all, tell yourself that boot camp is only for so many days; then it will be over with and life will be much more tranquil and enjoyable. Boot camp is only a hurdle, a goal that will come and be overcome. Say to yourself, "Why, I can put up with anything for that short a period of time." And . . . you will!

By being fully prepared physically and mentally you'll be way ahead of the average recruit, who arrives bewildered and perplexed. It's a miracle how a lot of these unprepared recruits make it through boot camp. But in your case it will be the result of foresight, groundwork, and advance preparation.

Some Common Activities

Every service's boot camp is conducted differently, but there are some activities and conditions that are common to all the boot camps.

First is the principle of "early to bed and early to rise." Reveille (wake-up) comes between 4:30 and 5:30 A.M., depending on the service and on the activities planned for the day. Usually some unpleasant wake-up music will be played on a loudspeaker, or a bugler will play the "reveille notes." As soon as you hear the first chords, it is wise to move—and move fast. You might have only a few minutes to get up, shave, arrange your bed and belongings, secure your valuables, and hit the road in formation.

Going to bed at about 9 P.M. is standard. It's not your choice, but remember that you don't have many personal choices in boot camp. This is the service's world. Later, after graduation from boot camp, your individual opinions and desires will be considered and respected. But not now.

Another common element is the demerit system. Discipline and standards are maintained by the instructor's issuance of demerits for infractions of the rules or regulations, or for failure to meet inspection criteria. Excessive demerits must be worked off (literally!) during free time. You'll be given "fun" jobs to do, like cleaning commodes, mowing grass in 105° heat, and so on.

As the weeks go by and you learn what to do and how to do it, and you show your instructor you can be responsible, the flow of demerits will slow or cease. Perhaps you might even receive a few merits, which are given for noteworthy acts or superior performance.

Training for men and women is integrated in the Air Force and the Coast Guard. It is separate in the Navy, Marines, and Army. Don't get the impression, though, that hanky-panky is allowed because of this mixed training. Living and housing arrangements are *not* integrated and, as all training is fast-paced and conducted under the watchful eyes of instructors and other servicepeople, fun and games are pretty much out of the question. Boot camp for both males and females is a time of challenge, hard work, and learning.

Off-duty Hours

Not all recruit training is work, however. Time is allowed for "liberty" beginning about the third week of training. There are two types of liberty. One allows you to leave the barracks area but stay on the base or post; the other is a full liberty that permits you to leave the base and sample the attractions of the local community. However, granting a recruit privileges and liberty is based on performance of duty.

You may not receive telephone calls during your training. If there is an emergency at home, your relatives should contact the nearest Red Cross for assistance. Pay telephones are available for your use as permitted during occasional free periods. You will be authorized one phone call during your first few days to advise relatives of your safe arrival.

Chapel attendance is supposedly voluntary, but sometimes those who don't go are stuck with work details. Unfair? Yes. You will find the Recruit Chapel offers a variety of religious services and styles of worship. There is a chaplain on duty at all times for personal counseling.

Military Time Clock

All the services have one thing in common: the way they tell time. The military has its own time system. The military clock runs on a 24-hour day. Hours of the day are numbered from 1 to 24. In the afternoon, instead of starting again with 1, the military goes to 13. The hours such as 8 A.M. or 7 P.M. are called 0800 (zero eight hundred) and 1900 (nineteen hundred), respectively. Hours and minutes in military time go like this: 10:45 A.M. is 1045 (ten forty-five); 9:30 P.M. is 2130 (twenty-one thirty).

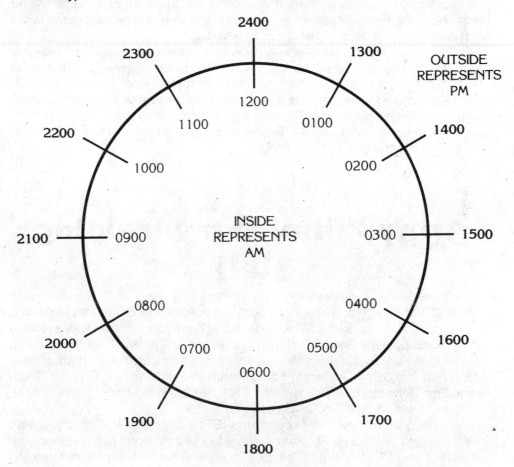

Military Time Clock
Figure 9-1.

A By-Service Description

We've talked about what boot camp is and what it isn't, about the importance of preparing yourself before arrival for training, and that there are some elements and activities common to all the boot camps. It is time now to find about how each of the services conduct their boot camps.

While many of the activities at boot camp are fairly standard and uniform in all the services, there are also many differences. You probably already have a good idea from this book that each service has a somewhat different idea about what it takes to be a good serviceperson. You won't be too surprised, for instance, to find that the Marines have the toughest and most physically challenging boot camp or that the Air Force is the most relaxed and easygoing. The other services vary. But these distinctions are by minor degree only, so don't get the mistaken notion that Air Force basic training will be a glorified summer camp for boys. If you do, you'll be in for a rude awakening.

All the services require self-discipline, teamwork, and tax your energies and mental capacities. All of them! The Marines may set higher physical standards, but the Air Force may compensate by inducing more mental stress and having a more burdensome academic load. It's difficult, then, to say for certain that the Air Force, Navy, or Army is "easier" or "easiest," and that Marine boot camp is the most demanding. It depends on the criteria you use.

The description given below of each service's boot camp was pieced together after visits to training centers for each service and after interviews with a great number of training instructors, other training center personnel, and new recruits. Also, I am indebted to the services for several excellent service publications used. Conditions do change, so some details may be different by the time you "hit the ground running" at boot camp. Nevertheless, I believe you'll find the following information both informative and useful.

Army Initial Entry Training (IET)

Army IET is what the soldiers call boot camp. It's conducted at any one of a number of Army installations. Which one you will go to depends on your eventual Military Occupational Specialty (MOS) and where you enlist. These boot camp sites include Fort Dix, New Jersey; Fort Jackson, South Carolina; Fort Knox, Kentucky; Fort McClellan, Alabama; Fort Leonard Wood, Missouri; Fort Sill, Oklahoma; Fort Benning, Georgia; and Fort Bliss, Texas. Women are trained only at Forts Dix, Jackson, and McClellan.

You'll leave for the seven-week-long Army IET by way of the AFEES. If you were in the Delayed Enlistment Program or there has been a lapse of time since your last visit to the AFEES, there will be some interviews to see if there have been any changes in your eligibility. An interviewer will ask you to report any medical or police problems you have had since your last visit to the AFEES. After they complete your records and orders, you're on your way, by bus or plane.

At the end of your ride you will find the Army reception station. As the name implies, this is where new soldiers are received into the training center. Normally, you can expect about a three-day stay at the reception station before picking up your new Army gear and being assigned to a training company.

The Reception Station

Before starting IET, each new enlistee undergoes reception station processing. This processing helps prepare new soldiers for training and later military life. During your brief stay at the reception station (normally three working days), you will live in reception station barracks and be supervised by reception station personnel.

Sufficient pay telephone facilities are provided at the reception station for you to call home if you desire (you may have to wait in line if they're busy). It might be advisable to tell your friends and family that you'll be pretty busy the first few days and that, if they don't hear from you right away, they shouldn't worry.

Reception station processing includes the following:

- Uniform issue and fitting
- Personnel records processing
- Identification card issue
- Immunization
- Eye and dental checks
- Pay
- Mental testing
- Interview
- Haircuts
- Orientation

The orientation will cover postal service, legal assistance, medical facilities, recreational facilities/activities, religious activities, leave and pass policies, post exchange facilities, medical care for dependents, financial care of dependents, movement of dependents, privately owned vehicles, visitors, family correspondence, shipment of civilian clothing, pay and allowances, service obligations, allotments, survivors' benefits, and Servicemen's Group Life Insurance. There will also be some classes in barracks upkeep, physical training (exercise), drill (marching), and other subjects that will help you adjust to Army living.

Now you're definitely in the Army!

Initial Entry Training

You've learned quite a lot during your three days at the reception station. Now you're going to learn even more about the Army—and yourself.

After testing the concept of men and women taking the same kind of training, the Army decided a common course of instruction for men and women was desirable. As a result of this decision, women can expect to receive essentially the same initial training as do men, although they will continue to be billeted separately. However, women are excluded from the more vigorous combat training that all men must undergo.

Physical Readiness Training

Physical Readiness Training has been modified for integration of men and women into the same program. The training consists of a variety of activities: running, calisthenics, and the obstacle course. The physical fitness test consists of push-ups, sit-ups, and running.

Classes

Both men and women can expect indoor and outdoor classes covering the following subjects:

- Military Courtesies and Customs
- Drill and Ceremonies
- ID and Wear of the Uniform
- Inspections
- Guard Duty
- Role of the Army
- Responsibility of a Soldier
- Code of Conduct, Geneva and Hague Conventions
- Marches and Bivouacs
- Basic Rifle Marksmanship
- Hand Grenades
- Familiarization with U.S. Weapons
- Personal Affairs (Service Benefits)
- Military Justice
- Equal Opportunity
- Hazards of Drug and Alcohol Abuse
- Personal Health and Hygiene
- Individual Protective Measures for Nuclear, Biological, and Chemical Defense
- First Aid
- Field Hygiene and Sanitation
- Individual Tactical Training Techniques
- Fire and Maneuver
- Defensive Training
- Confidence Course

Will it be tough? You bet it will, but if you're in reasonably good shape, the physical part of your training will be easier. But not too easy. If you did well in school, your classroom instruction will be easier. But not too easy. You'll use your muscles and your mind as you've never used them before. But if you try hard, you'll make it, as do a remarkably high percentage of the young people who come into the Army.

Your Sergeant

The sergeant is the primary individual responsible for your training during this period. You'll probably think that this individual does an unusual amount of shouting, all of which seems directed at you. But if it's any comfort, everyone in your training company feels the same way. Don't let it get to you.

A Week-by-Week Account

The weeks of Initial Entry Training are filled with training challenges and experiences you will never forget. The sequence of events may vary slightly at different posts, but the content will be generally the same everywhere. Some of the highlights you can expect are as follows:

First Week. Your training starts at a fast pace, but one you can handle. You do various exercises and run. You learn marching and facing movements, and start on the Manual of Arms with your new-found buddy, the M-16 rifle. You'll study the functioning of this weapon, how to sight-adjust, disassemble, and assemble. A drill sergeant will show you how to prepare for your first barracks inspection. And you'll learn that your first inspections are never good enough, but you'll get better.

During this week, you will also find yourself feeling better, despite some sore muscles and a few aches. More physical training—grass drills, various exercises, wind sprints, and running. And you'll be introduced to the obstacle course. Tough stuff, but it's great for building confidence. You'll take a physical fitness test to see how far you've come. One thing you'll realize is that you couldn't have done it a week earlier. The week will end with a preparation for a foot- and wall-locker inspection, including field equipment and clothing.

You won't be alone in training. You'll be a part of a group of persons—about 45 to 50—called a platoon. Your platoon members will be your friends and you'll want to work together as a team. If you—and they—don't, boot camp will be much tougher than it has to be.

Second Week. Most of this week will be spent on the firing range learning more about your M-16 rifle. You will receive lectures on firing-range procedures, coaching, steady-hold factors, and use of score cards. You'll also learn about sight adjustment, aiming point, and engaging surprise targets. There will be more training. Another inspection comes up, too, this time in formation without your weapon.

Third Week. Most of this week will also be spent on the firing range, practicing with your M-16. You will learn to fire from all positions, rapid reloading, and moving with a loaded weapon. You will also fire for record. Maybe you'll earn the badge of Marksman, Sharpshooter or Expert. You will make tactical daylight marches and bivouacs. And, just to keep you on your toes, a physical fitness test and weapons inspection.

You'll be weary and your muscles will still be sore, but somehow you'll feel better all over. The week ends with the inevitable inspection, this time in formation with your weapon.

Fourth Week. You will be outdoors all week and will experience night training. You'll also be introduced to grenades and how to use them. Big "stuff"—you'll have to follow instructions very carefully. You will also learn individual tactical techniques. Physical training gets tougher—longer runs, road marches, the obstacle course, the works. You'll get another test on what you've learned over the past week and, of course, another inspection.

Fifth Week. More night training, patrol and bivouac security. You will receive instruction in first aid and a general review of physical contact training exercises. You will learn that you don't dislike C-rations as much as you thought. The inspection this week consists of a field display on your bed in the barracks; foot and wall lockers; and in formation with your weapon.

Sixth Week. More tactical training, again mostly outdoors. You'll learn about additional weapons such as antipersonnel mines, antitank weapons, and grenade launchers. The interesting art of camouflage and its application on the battlefield will be taught and tested. All the while, you'll continue to become closer to your M-16 rifle.

Seventh Week. Are you the same person who signed the enlistment agreement? You're not. You are tougher, more disciplined, tired, perhaps, but you seem to be able to bounce back faster each day. During this week, you will review all you have learned and will be tested on it: combat proficiency, physical conditioning, and basic military knowledge. You'll wonder how you've learned so much in seven short weeks.

This is the wrap-up. All training and tests are completed. At the end of the week, you'll take part in the graduation exercises and pass in review before the commanding general. You've made it. You are now a well-trained, full-fledged soldier in the United States Army.

NAVY RECRUIT TRAINING COMMAND (RTC)

Departing from the AFEES, where there were last-minute medical checks and interviews, you'll arrive at a naval training center for boot camp, called Recruit Training Command (RTC) by our sea forces. The Navy has three different training centers, in Great Lakes, Illinois; San Diego, California; and Orlando, Florida. Often, men will be sent to the center nearest their home, but not always. All women are sent to Orlando, Florida, for RTC. As mentioned earlier, initial training for Marines and the Navy is not integrated by sex.

Receipt Day

Your day of arrival at RTC is called receipt day, the day when it seems as if your whole world has turned upside down. You'll be busy from the moment you arrive with initial processing and introductory instructions. You will then join other recruits and be formed into a company. You'll stay with these same individuals throughout boot camp and all of you will undoubtedly become a very close-knit, cooperative group. You'd better because, if you don't, things can get very difficult.

Physical Fitness

Almost from day one, you'll be concentrating on your physical fitness. There will be strenuous calisthenics and you'll be running two miles at a stretch by the time you graduate from RTC. If you arrive at RTC in poor physical condition, you might be given extra, or remedial, physical training.

To graduate from boot camp into the "real" day-to-day Navy, you will have to pass four different physical fitness tests. Each is more difficult than the first, but you'll be in better condition for each succeeding test.

As can be expected, the Navy is big on water skills. You will have to pass a test to demonstrate you can:

• Enter water feet-first from a height of five feet and float or tread water for five minutes. Sounds easy, but try it.

• Enter water in the deep end of a pool and swim 50 yards, using any stroke, keeping your head above the water.

• Practice techniques for preparing, and using, clothing and buoyant objects for staying afloat. (You'll be taught this).

Your First Days in the Navy

You'll spend your first few days at RTC getting organized. You'll be issued bedding and your Navy clothing, and fill out a multitude of forms. You'll be given a "chit book," which consists of coupons you can use at the Navy exchange stores to purchase needed toiletry items, postage stamps, pens, pencils, and paper. Later, this will be deducted from your first paycheck.

Naturally, you'll be fed, and you'll probably be surprised at how good the food is. For breakfast, the dining hall will heap on eggs, hot cakes, beef or bacon strips, ham, and fruit. For lunch and supper, there's everything from pizza to steak, with all the trimmings. The Navy figures you're working hard in boot camp and therefore need hearty meals. Believe it or not, some recruits even gain weight during RTC. Eating three square meals a day can do that to you.

One of the things you will miss while at RTC will be your hair (in addition, of course, to Mom, your girlfriend or boyfriend, and your hometown). Long hair is one of the first things to go. You'll be left with very short hair. You might learn to appreciate this because you won't have to worry about taking valuable training time to comb it. And remember, all your boot camp buddies will lose their hair, too, so you'll all be in the same boat. Don't worry, though; your first Navy haircut is the most severe. After that, you'll be allowed more and more hair growth. Of course, even at your first real duty station after RTC your hair may not be as long as it was when you were a civilian, but at least your shorn head won't spur roars of laughter.

Company Commanders

Your company will be composed of anywhere from 60 to 90 recruits, and you will have training instructors assigned to shepherd your group all the way through RTC. These training instructors are called company commanders, or CCs, by the Navy.

CCs know the Navy like the backs of their hands. They are probably better at instructing than the teachers you had in high school, and they are experts on leadership techniques. They'll teach you some basic facts about military customs and courtesies, marching and drill, and instruct you on Navy terminology. Your CCs will also show you how to maintain your military uniforms and the best way to keep the barracks in tip-top shape.

Your CCs are your immediate supervisors. These two or three noncommissioned officer/instructors have control over practically everything you do while in boot camp. They can be tough and demanding, but most have a ready ear and are willing to listen to any problems you wish to discuss. They'll make sure you meet the Navy's high standards, but they will also treat you fairly and be concerned about your welfare.

The Training Program

Recruit training will keep you extremely busy. The RTC consists of 380 formal sessions, 10 sessions per day.

Training instruction covers three general areas: naval and military training, technical training, and administration and processing.

Naval and Military Training. This consists of a number of subjects. For one thing, there's the Navy's organization, its mission, and the many regulations you need to know to succeed as a sailor.

Technical Training. There are many basic things every sailor must learn. This is true no matter what his or her specialty. Classes will be given in general seamanship, firefighting, chemical-nuclear-biological warfare and defense, and weapons and ordinance. Also, you'll be given information on the history of sea power, military justice, and the military pay and benefits system.

Here is a list of some of the classes and subjects you'll be taught:

- Accident Prevention
- Aircraft Familiarization
- Basic Seamanship
- Chain of Command
- Drill and Ceremonies
- Education Benefits
- Financial Responsibility
- First Aid
- History of the Navy
- Honors and Ceremonies
- Inspections
- Laws of War
- Leave, Liberty and Conduct Ashore
- Officer Recognition
- Personal Hygiene
- Security
- Ship Familiarization
- Survival at Sea
- Time Management
- Military Justice

Administration. During these periods you'll be fitted into the Navy, at least as far as the paperwork is concerned. You'll be certified medically and dentally fit, obtain an ID card, receive job-classification interviews, have your personal record established, and make out a service life insurance policy.

The Typical Training Day

Here's what a typical day at RTC will be like:

Morning:	0530	Reveille (wake-up)
	0530—0720	Clean up barracks; eat breakfast
	0720—1120	Training periods (indoor and outdoor)
Afternoon:	1120—1300	Lunch
	1300—1700	Training periods (indoor and outdoor)
Evening:	1700—1800	Dinner
	1800—1930	Shower, shave, shine shoes, arrange personal area
	1930—2015	Clean up barracks
	2015—2110	Study, write personal letters
	2110—2125	Last-minute instructions, night bunk check
	2125—2130	Tattoo (preparation for taps)
	2130	Taps (lights out). Everyone in bed

This is a typical day during the first weeks of RTC. As training proceeds, there'll be more time off in the evenings for relaxation and personal interests—but not that much more time off.

Service Week

Everyone's heard of KP duty. Well, in the Navy, and in RTC, this kind of detail is called "ship's work week" (SWW) training. You'll have the "opportunity" during SWW to perform KP (food service duties) in the dining facility, swab decks, mow lawns, or do other necessary but menial labor jobs that have to be done. Grin and bear it; it will pass.

Your Personal Affairs

When you report for training, your parents or next of kin will receive notice of your address. You will not need civilian clothing, so it will be stored at the recruit training center. You cannot receive telephone calls; but after the first week or two, you may make long-distance collect calls during off-duty time. No visitors are allowed during training, except on graduation day. On graduation day, you can invite your parents and friends. Your parents will dine in the enlisted persons dining facility with you on this final day of RTC.

Mail. Your CC will encourage you to write to your family and friends as soon as possible after you arrive. Tell your mail carrier at home not to forward third-class mail (newspapers, magazines) to you during recruit training because you will be too busy to read them and they'll require a change of address when you depart. Also, there's no place at RTC to store them.

Religion. The Navy offers a number of religious services. All training centers have chapels in which Catholic, Jewish, and Protestant services are conducted by chaplains. The chaplains make themselves available for pastoral counseling.

Liberty and Leave.   Only on graduation day will you be granted liberty. On completion of training, including your apprenticeship program, you will normally be allowed to take leave on the way to your first duty station.

Graduation Day

Finally, there's a pass in review (ceremony) on graduation day. You'll be handed a set of orders for your technical training or permanent base. You've passed that first obstacle. Now there are new adventures waiting, new people to meet, and new things to learn. Feel proud and walk tall—you're in the Navy!

AIR FORCE BASIC TRAINING (BT)

Airmen call their boot camp "basic training" (BT), or just "basic." It's conducted on a sexually integrated basis at only one location, Lackland Air Force Base in San Antonio, Texas. Lackland is called the "Gateway to the Air Force."

You'll arrive at Lackland probably by air, after receiving last-minute processing at the AFEES. An Air Force bus will transport you from the San Antonio airport to Lackland, where you and the other recruits on the bus will be dropped off at the Personnel Processing Center. This is where your six weeks of basic training begin.

Here, you'll be assigned to the basic Air Force unit—the flight—along with 40 or 50 other persons. They'll be your buddies for six weeks—some for life. You'll train with them, work with them, sweat with them, depend on them, and laugh with them. You'll develop a feeling of brotherhood with these persons, a camaraderie that comes from working together.

Teamwork is fundamental in basic. For example, half the flight will pick up the laundry while the other half makes up the bunks. Later, you'll find another kind of teamwork—along a flight line, for example. One person orders a jet engine, while several others install it.

Once you've been assigned to a flight, you're marched to a dining hall for a hot meal. The food will surprise you. You'll find soups, salads, meats, vegetables, desserts, ice cream, bread, butter, milk, tea, coffee, and soda. And if you're not too hungry, there are sandwiches, hamburgers, and french fries. You'll have meals like this each day during basic training; and you can eat and go back for seconds or thirds.

The Training Instructor (TI)

After your meal you'll meet your training instructor. The TI is tough and sharp. He had to pass a screening committee and complete an intensive eight-week school and 320 hours of classroom instruction and practical exercises.

The TI will have a partner who may or may not be with him. They'll spend the next six weeks of basic training with you. One of them will be with you at all times during the first 72 hours. They'll get to know your name, your personality, and something about your background. They'll tell you why things should be done and help you do the things you thought you couldn't.

Where You Will Live

Your TI will finish explaining the ground rules to you and you'll go to the dormitory where you'll live for the next six weeks. It's air-conditioned and comes complete with a mailroom, laundry room, classroom, supply room, television room, cafeteria, dispensary, offices, showers, beds, bays, and a large training area beneath the building. You can train here when it rains, or when it's too hot to train in the sun.

It's a little city within itself. Two-thirds of all basic trainees live in these dorms. The rest are housed in comfortable, renovated barracks buildings. Compared to conditions in the other services, the Air Force dormitories are "heaven."

Moving In

You'll get your blankets and linen and personal belongings and find your bunk. Half of your flight will take one bay, half will take another. Each TI will supervise a bay. The bays have eight showers, 12 sinks, latrines, a television day room, the TI's office, and a bulletin board. It's spotless and has to be that way. The TIs know this, but you don't. Leave 25 guys to clean up after themselves and see how the bay looks after one week.

You and your buddies will clean the latrines each morning. But right now it's 9 P.M. and you're entitled to seven and one-half hours sleep each night during basic training. The only time you won't get that much sleep is when you pull dormitory guard or student details. And that's not very often. The TI tells you he'll get you up in the morning, then turns out the light. You're on your way through basic training.

The First Week

Air Force basic training is a hectic, fast-paced six weeks, probably the fastest six weeks of your life. The first training week will be one of the biggest adjustments for you. Everything will come at you fast—new words and the tone in which they are said—or shouted. There will be new sights to see. It will seem like you have a million things to learn. Don't let it rattle you, though. More than 70,000 men and women, from all walks of life, graduated last year. They will tell you that basic was the best time of their life—once they got past the first week!

In this first week, the days are busy. You'll have rules to learn, records to start, and people to meet. You'll get paid, get a haircut, take a reading test, a language test, a blood test, and a hearing test. You'll get a medical examination, your eyes will be checked, and your teeth X-rayed. You'll learn to make your own bed, fold your clothes, arrange your closet, and wear the uniform. You'll learn to use new words like *dispensary, commissary, latrine, service cap, 1505 trousers,* and *flight*. And you'll get an orientation from your TI, the commander, the legal officer and the chaplain. You'll get up every morning at 5 A.M. and be in bed every night at 9 P.M., except on weekends.

And that's not all. You'll be issued uniforms and have them hand-fitted. And you'll confirm the location and length of your Air Force school if you enlisted for guaranteed training; or, if you enlisted for a specific aptitude index (mechanical, administrative, general, electronic), you'll select your Air Force job, one that will take you somewhere in the Air Force or back into civilian life with a usable skill. You will do all this in the first week.

The Rest of Basic

What about the rest of basic training? Basic training is divided into four parts: in-processing, military training, academic training, and evaluation. They all blend into one another from one week to the next.

Physical Training (PT).   Physical conditioning begins slow, but you'll be jogging a mile in eight minutes before you leave. And you'll do other calisthenic exercises and drill for two hours each day, so expect to be in great shape by graduation day.
In the Field.   You will familiarize yourself with a rifle and run a confidence (or obstacle) course. The Air Force does not emphasize combat skills as much as the other services, so this portion of your training won't be too difficult.

Classroom Training.   During basic, much of your time will be devoted to classroom instruction. You'll learn about customs and courtesies, Air Force history, first aid, and the organization and mission of the Air Force. There'll be many other subjects you'll be taught—see the Army and Navy boot camp sections (pp. 110 and 115) for a general idea. You'll be tested on this information, but to pass is not all that difficult if you study hard.

Drill.   If you've ever been a member of a high school band or perhaps a Junior ROTC or Civil Air Patrol Unit, you'll be way ahead in this department. If not, don't fret. Your training instructor will teach you, step by step, how to march and parade. And you'll get a lot of practice!

Graduation

On your last day of training, you'll hit the parade field one more time for a final review. Then, it's over and you've made it. You shake hands with your squadron commander and your TI. Your orders for school or that first duty assignment are waiting for you. Usually, you will be allowed to take leave time; however, if the opening date of your school class doesn't enable you to take leave, you will be given time off to go back home to visit the folks later on in school. In any case, basic is behind you and you can be proud of your achievement.

MARINE BOOT CAMP

Let's be blunt. After a few hundred years, the Marines are still . . . well, they're still the Marines. Training doctrine changes very slowly for the U.S. Marine Corps. This is particularly true of Marine boot camp. If Air Force boot camp is the easiest, there's no doubt that Marines have it the hardest. And with their all-out combat role, it's probably just as well that they do. In the office of some Marine drill instructors there is a plaque hanging on the wall that about says it all:

Sweat now in perspiration,
And you won't pay later in blood!

There are two Marine boot camps. Persons from east of the Mississippi go to Parris Island, South Carolina, and all other recruits are trained at San Diego, California.

When you step off the bus at either Parris Island or San Diego, you know immediately that your happy civilian life has come to an abrupt end. The drill instructor (DI) is the end-all and be-all for his recruits. He's sharp and trained to make *you* sharp—and he's got nearly eleven weeks to do it.

Women have a separate program for basic training, and though they have it easier than do the men, the Marine Corps is able to impart to the females that special brand of pride, spirit, and toughness that is the Marine trademark. Boot camp for women Marines lasts nine weeks, two less than for the men. Much of the combat training and physical regimen is cut out of the women's program and that accounts for the difference from the men's training.

The First Weeks

After your DI's warm initial greeting, you'll be made a part of a platoon, the basic training unit. You and the other members of your platoon will have little time for yourselves this first week. It will be go, go, go, all at the pleasure of the DI. You will get up at 5 A.M. and be in bed at 9 P.M.—your DI will make sure of that.

The Marine barracks (dormitories) are open-bay types. No one has an individual room; everyone lives together in one large space. You'll be taught how to keep your barracks clean, and you'll learn that even a speck of dust or lint won't be tolerated.

The Marines emphasize physical fitness, rifle skills, and combat training. You'll get a lot of practice in shooting the rifle during boot camp, and you'll be taught to kill. You'll learn to use the bayonet and learn, also, some hand-to-hand fighting. All this could save your life some day, should you ever land on a beach and have to face a well-trained enemy soldier with his own rifle and bayonet.

You can expect to run several miles a day plus be subjected to strenuous calisthenics. The Marine DIs are of the opinion that even this isn't enough, so when you make some kind of mistake, they are quick to demand, "Give me 20!" This means 20 push-ups, which you will do post-haste under the DI's watchful eye. This can be called extra, or "bonus," calisthenics.

The first weeks are the hardest. You'll be screamed at and you'll begin to think you made one big mistake when you got off that bus. But time will fly and things will get easier. And it's not all kill–kill–kill, drill–drill–drill, run–run–run and exercise. There will also be classes in first aid, customs, courtesies, history, the mission and organization of the Marine Corps, and a score of other subjects.

Free Time

Like boot camp in the other services, after you have proved yourself the first few weeks, things will get easier and some free time will come your way. Saturday afternoon and Sunday will be your time to relax and prepare for the coming week, unless, of course, you have excessive demerits for such infractions as deficiencies on an inspection, failure to salute, or being late. Often, you'll have to work off your demerits by performing menial tasks on the weekend, such as mowing grass, handling a mop, or painting. If so, goodbye town pass!

Graduation Day

Again, as in other services, there's a final review/parade on your last day of training, and then you'll be on your way home on leave for a well-deserved rest. The folks back home, especially your old buddies and friends, will make fun of your close haircut, but what do they know? They're not Marines. *You are!*

COAST GUARD RECRUIT TRAINING (RT)

Just a few short words on Coast Guard boot camp, called Recruit Training (RT). First of all, like the Air Force, Coast Guard training is conducted at only one recruit training center, in Cape May, New Jersey.

Second, the Coast Guard is very attuned to the women's rights movement and does its best to provide equal opportunity. It promotes integration by training men and women together. This doesn't mean they live together, only that their training is integrated just like a co-ed high school or a mixed sports team.

Boot camp for the Coast Guard is about nine weeks long and is no bed of roses. The work of the Coast Guard on the sea, in small boats, can be demanding. Coast Guard personnel must be capable of handling craft in choppy, dangerous waters, rescue people from drowning, and be able to perform strenuous physical labor while on board ship. Therefore, one of the goals at boot camp is to make you physically fit. Invariably, this is a goal that gets accomplished.

Naturally, swimming skills and water survival knowledge are basic components taught in boot camp. These are skills and techniques that you may some day, in an emergency on the high seas, appreciate, so this training is conducted in a deadly serious manner.

Like recruits in the other services, Coast Guard enlistees are taught to march and parade, maintain their uniforms and themselves immaculately, and practice the basics of self-discipline. There are also classes taught in seamanship ordinance and Coast Guard history. Teamwork is also emphasized.

You'll find that, while in peacetime it falls under the jurisdiction of the Department of Transportation, the Coast Guard is a legitimate part of our national security forces. A few people have made the mistake of joining the Coast Guard because they thought it would be fun. They imagined that water sports and recreational boating were a way of life in this service. Indeed, they may have decided that the Coast Guard wasn't really a part of the military. Boot camp quickly brought these mistaken recruits back to reality. The Coast Guard *is* a military force, and many Coast Guard personnel have given their lives for their country, both in peacetime and in war. So keep in mind the important mission of the Coast Guard, endure the rigors of boot camp, and graduate nine weeks later as a proud member of the U.S. Armed Forces.

Graduation

Hooray! Graduation Day. The day you graduate from boot camp will be one of the happiest and proudest moments of your life. You'll participate in a parade and review, and the marching will be so simple for you, you'll wonder why you ever worried that you'd never learn how. Your instructor will be all smiles, although you may not know whether he's happy for you and your buddies in the group or because he's happy that you're leaving. But whichever is the case, it's a happy occasion. You'll feel ten years older and twenty years more mature, and you'll be ready to learn that job skill you enlisted for and take your place in one of the most—if not *the* most—important professions in the United States of America.

10. Opportunities For Advancement

Everybody wants to get ahead. Advancing in your military career (even in a two-, three- or four-year career, if that's your intention) means increased pay, greater responsibilities, more status, and recognition. Some of the questions we'll answer in this chapter are:

- What is "rank" in the military?
- What rank can I expect to achieve?
- How does a person get promoted to a higher rank?
- Which service is the most generous in promoting its people to higher rank?

WHAT IS RANK?

Rank in the military is a term used to describe the level of achievement a person has attained. The military is a pyramidal, or hierarchical, organization. Everyone has a boss immediately above him or her in the pyramid. At the top of the pyramid is the President of the United States. Under our Constitution, he is the Commander-in-Chief of the Armed Forces. At the next step down on the pyramid is the civilian Secretary of Defense, who supervises the general in charge of each military service.

As a beginning enlisted person, you will, of course, be way down the pyramid. It will seem that everyone outranks you—is higher in the pyramid—but keep in mind that after your first day of boot camp, there will also be people behind you in the pyramid. In the military, people of the same rank distinguish themselves by seniority. So if you enter the Navy as a seaman recruit (E-1) on Wednesday, you'll be higher in rank than the person who enters and becomes a seaman recruit on the following Thursday. In effect, then, your rank lets everyone else in uniform know where you stand in the pyramid—that is, how you compare with everyone else.

In the military, telling who's in charge and who outranks whom is easy. All you have to do is look at the insignia a person has on his uniform. The charts shown in Figure 10-1 (Enlisted) and Figure 10-2 (Officer) provide insignia information for each service and rank. Note that, generally, the more stripes a person has on his arm, the higher rank that person has.

COMPARABLE MILITARY RANKS AND INSIGNIA

NAVY	MARINES
CAPTAIN	COLONEL
CAPTAIN	COLONEL
COMMODORE (WARTIME ONLY)	BRIGADIER GENERAL
COMMODORE	GENERAL
REAR ADMIRAL	MAJOR GENERAL
ADMIRAL	GENERAL
VICE ADMIRAL	LIEUTENANT GENERAL
ADMIRAL	GENERAL
ADMIRAL	GENERAL
ADMIRAL	GENERAL
ADMIRAL OF THE FLEET	(NONE)
ADMIRAL	
AS PRESCRIBED BY INCUMBENT ADMIRAL OF THE NAVY	(NONE)

ENLISTED MEN

SERVICE	ARMY	AIR FORCE	NAVY	MARINES
PAY GRADE E-1	(NONE)	(NONE)	SEAMAN RECRUIT	(NONE)
ADDRESSED AS	PRIVATE / PRIVATE	BASIC AIRMAN / AIRMAN	SEAMAN RECRUIT / SEAMAN	PRIVATE / PRIVATE
E-2	(NONE)	AIRMAN	APPRENTICE SEAMAN	PRIVATE FIRST CLASS
ADDRESSED AS	PRIVATE / PRIVATE	AIRMAN / AIRMAN	APPRENTICE SEAMAN / SEAMAN	PRIVATE FIRST CLASS / PRIVATE
E-3	PRIVATE FIRST CLASS	AIRMAN 1st CLASS	SEAMAN	LANCE CORPORAL
ADDRESSED AS	PRIVATE	AIRMAN	SEAMAN	LANCE CORPORAL
E-4	CORPORAL	SENIOR AIRMAN / SERGEANT	PETTY OFFICER 3d CLASS	CORPORAL
ADDRESSED AS	CORPORAL	SERGEANT	PETTY OFFICER	CORPORAL
E-5	SERGEANT	STAFF SERGEANT	PETTY OFFICER 2d CLASS	SERGEANT
ADDRESSED AS	SERGEANT	SERGEANT	PETTY OFFICER	SERGEANT
E-6	STAFF SERGEANT	TECHNICAL SERGEANT	PETTY OFFICER 1st CLASS	STAFF SERGEANT
ADDRESSED AS	SERGEANT	SERGEANT	PETTY OFFICER	SERGEANT
E-7	SERGEANT FIRST CLASS	MASTER SERGEANT	CHIEF PETTY OFFICER	GUNNERY SERGEANT
ADDRESSED AS	SERGEANT	SERGEANT	CHIEF	SERGEANT
E-8	1ST SGT / MSGT	SENIOR MASTER SERGEANT	SENIOR CHIEF PETTY OFFICER	1ST SGT / MSGT
ADDRESSED AS	SERGEANT	SERGEANT	CHIEF	SERGEANT
E-9	SERGEANT MAJOR	CHIEF MASTER SERGEANT	MASTER CHIEF PETTY OFFICER	SGT MAJOR / MGY SGT
ADDRESSED AS	SERGEANT	CHIEF	CHIEF	SERGEANT

OFFICERS

SERVICE	ARMY	AIR FORCE	NAVY	MARINES
			CHIEF WARRANT OFFICER W-4	
			CHIEF WARRANT OFFICER W-3	
			CHIEF WARRANT OFFICER W-2	
			WARRANT OFFICER W-1	
ADDRESSED AS ▶	MISTER	MISTER	MISTER	MISTER
	SECOND LIEUTENANT	SECOND LIEUTENANT	ENSIGN	SECOND LIEUTENANT
ADDRESSED AS ▶	LIEUTENANT	LIEUTENANT	MISTER	LIEUTENANT
	FIRST LIEUTENANT	FIRST LIEUTENANT	LIEUTENANT JUNIOR GRADE	FIRST LIEUTENANT
ADDRESSED AS ▶	LIEUTENANT	LIEUTENANT	MISTER	LIEUTENANT
	CAPTAIN	CAPTAIN	LIEUTENANT	CAPTAIN
ADDRESSED AS ▶	CAPTAIN	CAPTAIN	MISTER	CAPTAIN
	MAJOR	MAJOR	LIEUTENANT COMMANDER	MAJOR
ADDRESSED AS ▶	MAJOR	MAJOR	MISTER	MAJOR
	LIEUTENANT COLONEL	LIEUTENANT COLONEL	COMMANDER	LIEUTENANT COLONEL
ADDRESSED AS ▶	COLONEL	COLONEL	COMMANDER	COLONEL

SERVICE	ARMY	AIR FORCE
ADDRESSED AS ▶	COLONEL	COLONEL
	COLONEL	COLONEL
ADDRESSED AS ▶	BRIGADIER GENERAL	BRIGADIER GENERAL
	GENERAL	GENERAL
ADDRESSED AS ▶	MAJOR GENERAL	MAJOR GENERAL
	GENERAL	GENERAL
ADDRESSED AS ▶	LIEUTENANT GENERAL	LIEUTENANT GENERAL
	GENERAL	GENERAL
ADDRESSED AS ▶	GENERAL	GENERAL
	GENERAL	GENERAL
ADDRESSED AS ▶	GENERAL OF THE ARMY	GENERAL OF THE AIR FORCE
	GENERAL	GENERAL
ADDRESSED AS ▶	AS PRESCRIBED BY INCUMBENT	
	GENERAL OF THE ARMIES	(NONE)
	GENERAL	

Enlisted Pay Grade

Within each of the military services there are nine enlisted (E-), four warrant officer (W-), and ten officer (O-) grades. Since this book is oriented toward the enlisted jobs, the following explanation will also be oriented toward the enlisted person, but the principle applies to the officer and warrant officer structure as well.

At the bottom of the enlisted scale is the pay grade E-1. Most enlisted personnel enter the service at this pay grade. In the various services the rank of E-1 would be private, seaman recruit, or airman basic, respectively. At the top of the enlisted scale is the pay grade E-9. The rank corresponding to pay grade E-9 would be: Army—command sergeant major or sergeant major; Navy and Coast Guard—master chief petty officer; Air Force—chief master sergeant; Marine Corps—sergeant major or master gunnery sergeant.

CATEGORIES OF RANK

Within the same service there is a legal break between E-3 and E-4. This is the division between two important groups, lower-ranking enlisteds and noncommissioned officers. In the Air Force, an E-4 can be either a noncommissioned officer, in which case he will go by the title of sergeant, or he will be of lower rank, a senior airman. A senior airman moves up to the rank of sergeant after one year of training and after completing the required management and professional instruction. The Marine Corps also requires management training for its NCO's.

You may have also noticed in the chart that the Army has the Specialists rank (Specialist 4, 5, and 6). Specialists are highly trained technicians and administrators whose primary function is not management and supervision. Even though they get paid according to their E- pay grade, the same as those in the equivalent pay ranks of corporal, sergeant, and staff sergeant, specialists are not noncommissioned officers. Indeed, just what is a noncommissioned officer?

Noncommissioned Officers (NCOs)

Most enlisted personnel in pay grades E-4 and above are noncommissioned officers. Without a doubt, the NCO Corps form the backbone of the military. This exceptionally well-skilled and dedicated bunch of pros makes the service click and makes sure the job gets done. Some have been in the service 10 years, others 20 or even 30 years. They are the leaders and supervisors who work in the "trenches" with their enlisted personnel, motivating, guiding, and assisting this vast personnel resource. Make no mistake about it, and learn it early in your career, the NCOs for whom you work can make you or break you.

When you get to your first permanent station, you'll undoubtedly find that your

NCOIC (NCO-in-charge) has only one thing in mind: to help you become a success. Your NCOIC will see to it that you get the training you need to do your job right, and he will be a source of knowledge which you can use when in need. Your NCOIC probably will even be there to counsel and guide you when you encounter severe personal problems.

However, if you don't perform as you should, if you are tardy to work, sloppy in dress, display a negative attitude, or otherwise become a burden to your unit, your NCOIC will come down hard on you. Invariably, your commanding officer will follow the advice of his NCOICs when it comes to meting out punishment to wrongdoers or underachievers.

Your NCOIC is the person who evaluates your performance and who recommends or does not recommend you for promotion. And, again, it is a wise commanding officer who listens to the advice and recommendation of his NCOIC.

What does this mean to you? Well, it means that to get ahead you will have to prove to your NCOIC that you are a capable and dedicated enlisted person. You can best do this by learning your job well and doing it well. That's all it takes. If you have a complaint or a suggestion on how to do the job better, tell your NCOIC. He wants you to be happy and he wants to improve working conditions. They can't always accommodate your desires or carry out your worthwhile suggestions, but they'll try.

Officers

Above the ranks of the NCO Corps is the category of officer. The rank of officers ranges from second lieutenant (ensign in the Navy) to general (admiral in the Navy). The second lieutenant has a gold bar (gold-plated actually) insignia, while the general has four stars. There is also the rank of five-star general, or admiral, but Congress has not awarded this rank since Douglas MacArthur, Dwight Eisenhower, and others of World War II fame held the rank.

There is also another category of officers, warrant officers. Their pay grades are W-1 through W-4. The warrant officer has neither the status nor the rank of the lowest O-1 pay-grade officer, the second lieutenant. Warrant officers are experts in a special skill/career area and exercise considerable management authority. However, they are limited in job assignment to their peculiar specialty, whereas other officers may be assigned to management positions over subordinates in any career field or specialty.

Warrant officers generally assume their status after having served as enlisted persons and proved they deserved warrant status. The Air Force is the only service that does not have warrant officers.

Officers constitute the upper-level managers of the armed forces. Even the lowest-ranking officer (O-1 or W-1) outranks the highest-ranking enlisted person (E-9). This is true regardless of the age of the persons holding either rank, their educational level, or any other criteria. In the following chapter, we'll discuss in much greater detail the difference between officers and enlisted personnel, and in Chapter 12 we'll talk about how a person can become an officer. But for now, it is enough to emphasize that officers are higher in rank than enlisted personnel, including NCOs, and that NCOs form the upper tier of the enlisted structure.

The following diagram depicts the rank structure of military personnel:

Officers (O-1 to O-10)

↓

Warrant Officers (W-1 to W-4)

↓

Noncommissioned Officers (E-4 to E-9)

↓

Enlisted (E-1 to E-4)

The Lower-Ranking Enlisted

If NCOs are the backbone of the armed forces, enlisted persons in grades E-1 through E-3 are the muscles because they are the ones who actually do most of the work. They are the ones who do the often grueling tasks that make our military the efficient and effective organization it is today. They are the "dogfaces," the "flyboys," the "grunts"—the guys, and now gals, without whom there would be no military.

Today they are also the clerk-typists, the computer operators, the tail gunners, the carpenters, the riflemen, the electricians, and the personnel specialists. So, along with the muscles come a lot of brains, too. Today's enlisted person is educated and talented and is treated as such.

Most lower-ranking enlisted have less than three years of service experience. By the time they have that much seniority, they are promoted to NCO status, if their performances are at least average in being up to speed.

PROMOTIONS: WINNING A HIGHER RANK

Most persons are awarded E-1 status on their first day of active duty. Some, however, receive higher rank. If you have a needed skill, have completed a three-year Junior ROTC program in high school, or participated in the Civil Air Patrol, you may be eligible to enter the service at the E-3 pay grade. You may also receive higher rank by taking advantage of other enlistment options.

Let's assume, though, that you start out as an E-1, as do most enlistees. How long will it be before you win higher rank? Indeed, how can you *keep* advancing up the ranks? As I said, higher rank denotes more responsibility and the attainment of a higher level of achievement; plus, it means more money in your pocket. Anyone who says he is not interested in higher rank is either lying, foolish, or both!

Each service has its own unique promotion system. To describe each one in detail would take up much more space than this book could possibly afford, so I've briefly described the key elements of each service's promotion system.

Air Force

An airman basic (E-1) is promoted to airman (E-2) upon completion of six months time-in-service. However, airmen who qualify under the six-year enlistment program, or are graduates of JROTC, or have received the Billy Mitchell Award through Civil Air Patrol participation are promoted to airman first class (E-3) after basic training. Airmen are normally promoted to E-3 after six months time-in-grade as an E-2, provided they are recommended by the commander and are progressing satisfactorily in training.

Promotion to senior airman (E-4) normally occurs at about the 33-month point, when members are fully qualified in their specialty and are recommended by their immediate commander. Up to this point, promotions are noncompetitive. A special program exists which allows outstanding airmen to compete for promotion to senior airman up to 12 months earlier than usual.

Appointments to sergeant (noncommissioned officer status, E-4, which does not constitute a change in pay or benefits) occurs one year after promotion to senior airman and after completion of professional military education.

Airmen are eligible for promotion to staff sergeant and higher grades after completing time-in-grade and service requirements, completing required promotion tests, having the commander's recommendation, and qualifying in their specialty for higher grades. These promotions are competitive, and the Air Force promotion system shows members how they stand in relation to their contemporaries.

Army

After completing six months of active service, a private E-1 is advanced to private E-2. Promotion to private first class (E-3) requires 12 months of active service, four months of time-in-grade as an E-2, and the commander's approval. To meet requirements for promotion to E-4, the individual must have 24 months of service, six months of time-in-grade as an E-3, and the commander's recommendation. In exceptional cases, the commander may accelerate promotions to E-3 and E-4.

Eligibility for promotion to E-5 and E-6 requires the individual to compete by Military Occupational Specialty category using standardized criteria under the Army's 1,000-point system. Some of the qualifications are full proficiency in the job skill in which the promotion will be made, recommendation from the commander, completion of time-in-grade and service requirements, a qualifying Skill Qualification Test score, and high school diploma or GED equivalent. Waivers for certain criteria are authorized to allow well-qualified soldiers to advance more rapidly.

In addition to the above standards, promotion to grades E-5 and E-6 requires appearance before and selection by a board of officers and noncommissioned officers. Promotion to E-7 through E-9 is centralized and requires selection by Department of the Army boards. The number of promotions made to grades E-5 through E-9 is controlled monthly by the Department of the Army.

Coast Guard

A Coast Guard seaman recruit (E-1) is promoted to seaman apprentice (E-2) upon completion of basic training.

Eligibility for promotion to seaman or firefighter (E-3) is based on adequate time-in-grade, demonstration of military and professional qualification, recommendation of the commanding officer, and completion of correspondence courses.

To earn petty officer ratings (E-4 through E-9), an individual must, in addition to meeting requirements already stated, pass the Coast Guard-wide competitive examination for the rating or complete service schooling. The Coast Guard has an accelerated program in which those having special training in needed skill areas are promoted to E-4 and E-5 immediately after recruit training.

Marine Corps

Advancement is determined by the manner in which Marines perform their duties and demonstrate their leadership potential. While the top ten percent of the privates graduating from recruit training may be meritoriously promoted by their commanding general, normal promotion is received after six months of service, unless the Marine qualifies for an accelerated promotion through an enlistment option.

All Marine Corps promotions are competitive, based upon subjective evaluation of the Marine's performance. The Marine's commanding officer governs promotions through lance corporal; promotions to the noncommissioned officer (NCO) ranks (corporal to sergeant) are quite selective and based upon the needs of the service. Normally the time-in-grade requirement for promotions to lance corporal and corporal is eight months; promotion to sergeant generally requires 12 months of time-in-grade. Promotions above the rank of sergeant into the staff NCO ranks have various time-in-grade requirements, based on the needs of the service.

Navy

A Navy seaman recruit (E-1) is advanced to seaman apprentice (E-2) upon completion of six months of active duty, with the commanding officer's recommendation.

Eligibility for advancement to seaman (E-3) is based on requirements for adequate time-in-grade, demonstration of military and professional qualifications, passage of local examinations, and recommendation of the commanding officer. For advancement to the petty officer ratings (E-4 through E-9), an individual must fulfill the minimum time-in-service and grade; complete training, correspondence courses or service schooling; demonstrate military and professional qualifications; be recommended by the commanding officer; pass the Navy-wide competitive examination for the rating; and pass the Navy-wide competitive military requirements tests (E-4 and E-5 only).

Advancement to E-4 through E-6 is based on a final multiple, which is determined through points earned for awards, total active service, time-in-grade, performance marks for duty, and examination scores. For advancement to E-7 and above, individual records are reviewed by the Department of the Navy. Final selections are made by a board. Advancements, determined by vacancies in each career field, are then made in order from the highest multiple to the lowest.

HOW ABOUT YOU?

What is most important about the military promotion system is how it affects you. Sure, the descriptions given provide some help in explaining how the services promote deserving people, but the question still remains, how can *you* assure promotion. How can *you* get ahead by advancing to higher rank? And beyond this basic question is another, just as significant: how can you win *accelerated* promotion?

The Army: Winner Hands Down!

There are really two answers to these questions. First, you can better assure yourself of being promoted as rapidly as possible by choosing a service that promotes faster than the others. You see, contrary to what many civilians and even quite a few people in service think, there is no common "advancement times" among the services. In fact, there is a pronounced difference in the degree of generosity each service displays in handing out higher rank.

This difference in promotion opportunity can be seen in Figure 10-3, which depicts promotion timing for each service. This chart, prepared in 1982, shows how many years you will have to stay in the respective service before you win promotion to the rank listed. Keep in mind that this is how long it takes the *average* enlisted person to be promoted to the rank. Some persons get promoted sooner, some later, depending on performance.

This chart tells us several things. First, it tells us that the Army is the grand winner in the promotion business up to E-4 and the Navy isn't far behind. In the Army, the average soldier is promoted to the rank of corporal (E-4) in 1.80 years. That works out to about one year and nine months. However, the average Navy fellow will have to wait several months more to make E-4. Lagging behind even more is the Marine and the Air Force person, who has to wait about two and a half years to make E-4 rank.

Interestingly, E-5 comes at about the same time for all the services, all except the Air Force. While seamen, soldiers, and Marines can make E-5 in about three years and nine months or so, the hapless airman has to wait for over five years! The time for E-6 is about seven years for all the services, but it'll take the poor airman over 12 years to become a technical sergeant (E-6)!

The Army also promotes lower-ranking officers faster. An Army second lieutenant (O-1) can make rank of first lieutenant (O-2) in only a year and a half, and two years later—after three and a half years—he will be a captain (O-3). The equivalent rank in the other services takes two years for O-2 and four years for O-3. However, the Marine officer must wait four years and and ten months to be an O-3.

These figures point out that if rapid advancement is your greatest priority, then perhaps you should consider joining either the Army or the Navy. But the opportunity to achieve higher rank as quickly as possible may not be as important to you as some other considerations. If you've checked out what each service has to offer in terms of life-style, jobs, training and education, and other alternatives, any or all of these may weigh heavier in your choice of service than promotion opportunities.

Also, it's well to remember that no matter which service you choose, and how quickly or slowly they promote, your own progress in rank depends on how well you perform your duties. If your boss—your NCO in charge—rates you highly in job performance and attitude, you can advance much faster than your contemporaries and peers.

Achieving a High Rating

All the services have provisions to promote people who show greater promise than the average soldier, Marine, airman, or sailor of equal time-in-service. Those people who shine—who do more than the minimum in their jobs and in training—can expect to be promoted ahead of everyone else. For instance, a "fast burner," as they are called, might be advanced to E-5 in as little as four years in the Air Force, while the average person takes over five years to achieve that rank. In the Army, the average enlisted person makes corporal (E-4) in about two years. Catch the eye of your military superiors as a "go-getter" and you'll be a corporal in a little over a year.

Evaluation

All enlisted persons are given frequent evaluations by their superiors. This evaluation can take the form of a letter written by the supervisor to a promotion board, detailing the individual's achievements (or, conversely, his failure to achieve), or a formal evaluation report. A formal evaluation is a document or form completed by the NCO supervisor at regular intervals that describes the way the person has accomplished his duties. An example of the evaluation report used by one service (the Air Force) is shown in Figure 10-4a and 10-4b).

The formal evaluation report is of utmost importance in the rating process. If the supervisor describes the person's performance as substandard or lacking in some respects, such comments can severely hurt that person's promotion chances. Because these reports are so important to an individual's career, usually the supervisor's ratings and evaluation have to be agreed on by other persons higher in the rank structure. This is sort of like getting a second or third opinion, although the evaluation by the first—or immediate—supervisor is rarely challenged.

A series of exceptionally good evaluation reports can propel you straight up the ladder. On the other hand, if you consistently receive negative reports, you may find your promotion chances either dim or nil.

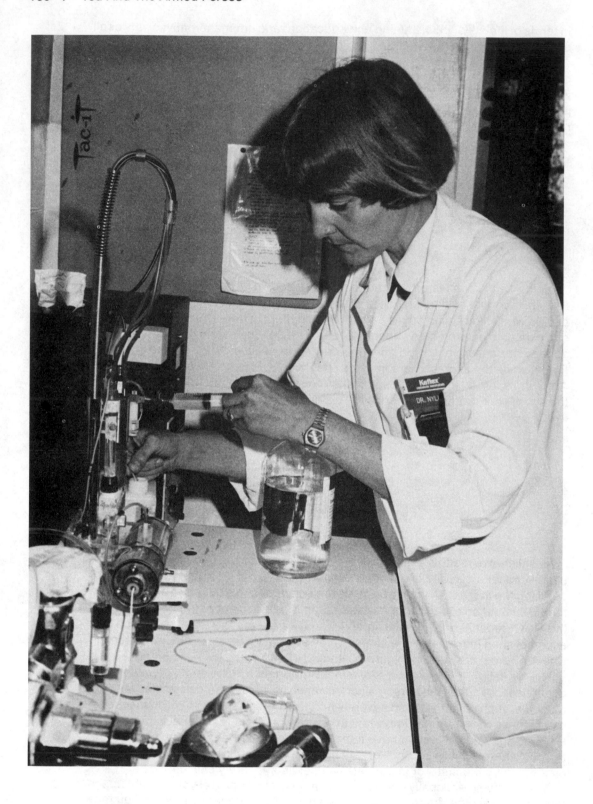

It's Not Who You Know!

One advantage of the military promotion system is that everyone has an equal opportunity to achieve higher rank. In the service, it doesn't matter who you know, where you come from or what your family's social status is.

In the civilian workworld, the man who gets ahead is often the one who knows somebody. If a person's father, uncle, brother, or cousin is the president of the company or in a high and powerful position, he can reasonably expect to move up the ladder of success. This is often true regardless of how well (or how poorly) the person performs his job.

Likewise, being descended from a family of great social distinction might help a person gain employment with a firm and receive frequent promotion. Also, some civilian companies and corporations give a lot of credence to those who graduated from a prestigious school or university.

None of these undemocratic and perhaps unfair criteria are used by the military as the basis for either entrance or advancement. Everyone has the same opportunity to enlist and get ahead. In the military services only one criterion is used, and that is how well someone does his duties.

By evaluating a person's performance strictly on its merits, the military services are truly demonstrating the American ideal of fairness and equal opportunity, and this benefits the military because the most dedicated and capable individuals are selected for higher rank. As you can see, your opportunity for advancement in the military depends on only one person—*YOU*.

Time-in-Service at Promotion (Enlisted)

Grade	Army	Navy	Marine Corps	Air Force
E-9	22.42	20.74	22.30	22.95
E-8	18.56	17.53	18.35	19.65
E-7	12.65	13.43	11.68	16.22
E-6	7.65	7.32	7.20	12.13
E-5	3.80	3.70	3.68	5.29
E-4	1.80	2.08	2.48	2.56
E-3	1.01	1.26	1.17	.84
E-2	.55	.55	.55	.47

(Years are rounded off to hundredths; e.g., .50 would equal 6 months)

Figure 10-3.

I. RATEE IDENTIFICATION DATA	(Read AFR 39-62, Vol I, carefully before completing any item.)			

1. NAME (Last, First, Middle Initial)
Monroe, James L.

2. SSAN 220-71-0318

3. GRADE A1C

4. ORGANIZATION, COMMAND, LOCATION AND PAS CODE
47th Equipment Maintenance Squadron (TAC) Luke AFB, AZ

5. PERIOD OF REPORT AND SUPERVISION
FROM 1 Aug 81
THROUGH 31 Jul 82

NO. OF DAYS 150

6. REASON FOR REPORT
☒ CHANGE OF RATER
ANNUAL
DIRECTED BY

7. PAFSC 43151C **8. DAFSC** 43151C **9. CAFSC** 43151C

II. JOB DESCRIPTION: RF-4C Jet Aircraft Phase Inspection Specialist. Performs inspections and preventive maintenance on RF-4C aircraft, including hourly postflights, periodic and engine bay. Insures compliance with all prescribed technical data, and time change components. Removes, adjusts, troubleshoots and installs aircraft system replacement parts. Services, operational checks, inspects aircraft air/pneudralic systems. Cleans airframe, identifies corrosion and if necessary, prepares condition tags for parts turn-in. Assists in ground handling, fueling, defueling and aircraft trim pad maintenance runs. Operates powered and non-powered aerospace ground equipment.

III. EVALUATION OF PERFORMANCE

1. PERFORMANCE OF DUTY — RATER: 9; 1ST INDORSER: 9
2. HUMAN RELATIONS — RATER: 9; 1ST INDORSER: 9
3. LEARNING ABILITY — RATER: 8; 1ST INDORSER: 8
4. SELF-IMPROVEMENT EFFORTS — RATER: 9; 1ST INDORSER: 9
5. ADAPTABILITY TO MILITARY LIFE — RATER: 9; 1ST INDORSER: 9
6. BEARING AND BEHAVIOR — RATER: 8; 1ST INDORSER: 8

IV. OVERALL EVALUATION
RATER: 9; 1ST INDORSER: 9; 2D INDORSER: 9; 3D INDORSER: (blank)

AF FORM 909 SEP 79 PREVIOUS EDITIONS ARE OBSOLETE.

AIRMAN PERFORMANCE REPORT (Airman Basic thru Senior Airman)

Figure 10-4a.

REVERSE SIDE OF AIRMAN PERFORMANCE REPORT

V. RATER'S COMMENTS FACTS AND SPECIFIC ACHIEVEMENTS: Since his assignment to the Phase Inspection Section, Amn Monroe has demonstrated a strong desire to learn all aspects of his job. Upon completion of his Aircraft Maintenance Training (AMT), he has proven to be an enthusiastic and productive mechanic and shows potential of being highly qualified in his field. His specific achievements include discovering several foreign objects in aircrafts and cockpits during a recent hourly post-flight inspection. Amn Monroe has displayed his concern for safety by eliminating the foreign objects that could have jammed flight controls and resulted in an aircraft mishap. His consistent search for foreign objects and discrepancies was a considerable contribution to an excellent inspection report given to the dock for their maintenance on aircraft. STRENGTHS: His friendly personalty and positive attitude makes it possible for Amn Monroe to work in difficult conditions with specialists and any member of his shop. EDUCATIONAL AND TRAINING ACCOMPLISHMENTS: It is noteworthy that Amn Monroe has recently completed the Effective Reading Course which lasted approximately eight weeks, on his own time. He has completed each volume of his specialty course in minimum time and with superior results. OTHER COMMENTS: Amn Monroe is active in squadron extracurricular programs and keeps himself physically fit. He deserves early promotion

NAME, GRADE, BRANCH OF SERVICE, ORGANIZATION, COMMAND AND LOCATION	DUTY TITLE	DATE
David A. Miller, SSgt, USAF 47th Equipment Maintenance Squadron (TAC) Luke AFB, AZ	Phase Dock Supervisor	31 July 82
	SSAN 250-70-6519	**SIGNATURE** David a. Miller

VI. 1ST INDORSER'S COMMENTS ☐ CONCUR ☐ NONCONCUR

I have observed this man's performance on a daily basis. His dedication and initiative have contributed greatly to the Phase Inspection Section. His attitude and willingness to accept orders from his superiors is a contribution to the mission of this organization and overall mission of the wing. His overall performance is noteworthy as dock inspection member.

NAME, GRADE, BRANCH OF SERVICE, ORGANIZATION, COMMAND AND LOCATION	DUTY TITLE	DATE
Howard Lewis, CMSgt, USAF 47th Equipment Maintenance Squadron (TAC) Luke AFB, AZ	NCOIC	31 July 82
	SSAN 467-38-1210	**SIGNATURE** Howard Lewis

VII. 2D INDORSER'S COMMENTS ☐ CONCUR ☐ NONCONCUR

Amn Monroe has the keen ability to take on a new challenge in an efficient manner. He is quick to obey orders and requests from his superiors and he does all that is asked of him in an excellent manner. Amn Monroe is an asset to the inspection section and contributes to its many excellent ratings given it.

NAME, GRADE, BRANCH OF SERVICE, ORGANIZATION, COMMAND AND LOCATION	DUTY TITLE	DATE
James Gordon, Capt, USAF 47th Equipment Maintenance Squadron (TAC) Luke AFB, AZ	Commander, 47th Equipment Maintenance Squadron	31 July 82
	SSAN 410-20-1612	**SIGNATURE** James Gordon

VIII. 3D INDORSER'S COMMENTS ☐ CONCUR ☐ NONCONCUR

THIS SECTION NOT USED

NAME, GRADE, BRANCH OF SERVICE, ORGANIZATION, COMMAND AND LOCATION	DUTY TITLE	DATE
	SSAN	**SIGNATURE**

Figure 10-4b.

11. Officer Versus Enlisted

In the social order in which one person is officially subordinated to another, the superior, if he is a gentleman, never thinks of it, and the subordinate, if he is a gentleman, never forgets it.

—General John J. Pershing
Commander, Allied Forces
World War I

Many civilians—perhaps most—don't have the foggiest notion that there is a difference between an enlisted person and an officer in the military service. Sure, they may have a vague understanding that generals and officers "run things," but just where petty officers, sergeants, lieutenants, colonels, and all the other ranks fit is a big mystery to them.

After reading the previous chapter, you know all about the various enlisted pay grades and ranks, and you have at least a fair understanding of the military rank structure. As you've seen, officers are on top as the overall managers, noncommissioned officers (NCOs) follow, and lesser enlisted persons—E-1 to E-4—fill the bottom ranks. Still, the question may spring up in your mind, *why* is there this difference? What makes an officer an officer?

This is a question that deserves to be answered. Recognizing the difference between officers and enlisteds, and the reason for this difference, will help you to be fully prepared mentally for the unique demands and discipline required by the services of their people. With this knowledge and preparation, you'll be a long step ahead of other recruits entering the service.

OFFICER PRIVILEGES

As I have discussed, the military is a hierarchical organization. In other words, power flows from the top down. Control is exercised by officers at the top level over enlisteds at lower levels, and, as we have seen, there are also sublevels of control and leadership within each group. The higher a person is in this hierarchy, the more privileges he will have, and the more the people lower on the totem pole will have to demonstrate their recognition of the person's superiority.

This is called "rank has its privileges" (RHIP) in the military. The services are set up to reinforce this concept of RHIP, and because everyone wears their rank either on the shoulder or the arm of their uniform, day in and day out, everyone is reminded of his own place in the overall pecking order.

Among the privileges of rank accorded officers are the salute, the use of the address "Sir" or "Ma'am," and respectful language and behavior by enlisteds. Also, an enlisted person must come to "attention"—a position of being erect and braced in posture—when directed by an officer. Another courtesy given the officer by enlisted people is to stand when a superior officer enters the room.

NCOs are not generally accorded these courtesies and signs of respect, except perhaps during boot camp. So it is apparent that officers are the superior group within the military organization. And the paying of proper respect to officers illustrates the fact that there is a vital difference between officers and enlisteds.

THE DIFFERENCE

The unequal relationship between military officers and enlisteds seems strange and out of place in our democratic society, yet the American military has always had a gap between the two groups. Even General George Washington's forces at Valley Forge were divided into officer and enlisted.

In addition to its historical roots, this gap is also firmly based in law. The Uniform Code of Military Justice, a set of laws passed by the U.S. Congress, sharply distinguishes between officers and enlisted. Service regulations codify this legal distinction and provide for different rules of behavior on the part of each of the two personnel groups. An officer, for example, is required to meet far higher standards of conduct than is an enlisted person.

An explanation is required as to why it is necessary to maintain this strict division between the two categories of personnel. What is the source of the difference?

Commission vs. Enlistment

One way to look at this difference is to study the varied way each of the two groups enters the military. If we do this, we find that enlisted persons are young men and women who seek to join, or enlist, in one of the services through a local military recruiter. The applicant generally holds a high school diploma, although some do not. In addition, the applicant must meet the service's minimum physical and mental standards. If these minimum standards are met and there is an opening or quota available, the applicant signs a contract to serve a period from two to six years. The next step is for the young person to be given an "oath of service" (be sworn in). With this oath, the person becomes a full member of the service and proceeds to basic training.

The officer, however, enters the military through a more difficult and arduous route. He also must meet certain minimum physical and mental standards. And, unlike enlisted applicants, officer hopefuls must, with few exceptions, be college graduates.

But meeting physical and mental standards and possessing a college degree is only the beginning. The officer candidate must next embark on and complete a comprehensive, and often very lengthy, officer training program. This program varies. Some candidates take on the four-year challenge of the military academies. Taking ROTC during the college years is another alternative, as are the fast-paced officer training schools run by each military service.

Whatever the source of the training, the officer candidate must successfully undergo a course of instruction that grooms and prepares him for leadership duty as an officer. In addition to the normal military and physical fitness regimen, instruction also includes management, leadership, and world affairs—subjects not taught the new enlisted recruit. The new officer thus enters military service prepared to meet supervisory and leadership challenges. This contrasts with the more limited perspective instilled in the enlisted basic training courses.

The candidate who successfully completes the officer training program takes an oath of office and is awarded a "commission." The commission is to the military officer what the license is to a doctor or lawyer. It entitles him to certain rights and privileges, but also demands a certain standard of ethical behavior and responsibility.

Enlisted personnel on active duty may apply to become officers, but they will have to meet all the officer prerequisites, including, in most cases, possession of an undergraduate college degree, and they will have to complete an officer training course. Each service accepts a limited number of its enlisteds into the officer ranks each year.

If an enlisted person does not meet these prerequisites, apply for a commission, or go through the officer training program, the person will remain in the enlisted ranks for as long as he remains in the service. This is the case even if the enlisted person's duty performance is superb, his record impeccable, and the enlisted person otherwise meets all qualifications for officer status. There is no such thing, except in times of war or in extremely unusual cases, as a *direct* commission.

Advanced Leadership Training

Throughout their careers, officers are trained by the military to assume leadership duties. Not only initial officer training, but subsequent advanced training courses as well emphasize the generalized managerial tasks of the officer corps. This compares with the more specialized training given enlisted personnel, training designed to foster obedience to orders and afford detailed knowledge of the technical, combat, or administrative duties typically engaged in by enlisted personnel.

The difference in training emphasis for officers is needed because of the higher level of management responsibility of the officer corps.

Type and Level of Responsibility

Probably the major difference between the two categories of personnel—enlisted and officer—has to do with the type of work each is assigned and the level of responsibility. Officers, as a group, are the upper-level managers and controllers of all activities and all work performed in the military.

Officers are the commanders of the ships, submarines, infantry units, tank groups, and flying squadrons. They lead, manage, and make the rules which everyone below them, lower-ranking officers and enlisted alike, must follow. In civilian life, they would be the chiefs of government agencies and directorates, and the teachers, professors, and other professionals. In the military, pilots are officers, as are doctors, lawyers, chaplains, and scientists. Officers, then, represent the upper stratum of military society—the elite, that is.

Enlisted personnel, on the other hand, are to the military what skilled and unskilled laborers and technicians are to the civilian workworld. Combat soldier, combat Marine, tank driver, aircraft maintenance specialist, hospital lab technician, plumber, carpenter, driver, electrician—all of these are enlisted. Enlisted people paint ships and offices, repair roads and telephone lines, fix faulty heaters and air conditioners, type and file documents, and maintain missiles and jeeps. They parachute from planes and ride amphibious craft onto shore in battle.

In effect, enlisted people *do* and officers *supervise* what is done. As one airman said to me, "Enlisted people do the hard, dirty work; officers don't like to get their hands greasy." His comment was not entirely correct, but its intent was. Officers *do* work, but the work they do is different in degree and type than that of most enlisted personnel. It is true that officers rarely do manual labor; but many put in long hours to accomplish their jobs.

However, it is simplistic to say that officers do *all* the supervising or managing of the work in the services. Actually, there are also many supervisory people in the enlisted ranks.

Enlisted persons, by virtue of their experience, seniority, and knowledge can receive promotion to lower-level supervisory positions of significant responsibility. This first-level supervisory role is acknowledged by the term *non-commissioned officer*, or NCO, given to enlisted persons in the higher ranks. A good way to understand the various levels of supervision in the military is to roughly compare the job titles of military officers and enlisted personnel with those of civilian society. This comparison is made in Figure 11-1.

MILITARY vs. CIVILIAN TITLES

Military Rank	*Equivalent Civilian Titles*
High-ranking Officers: General, Admiral, and Colonel	Chief Executive, Director, President; Vice President, Chairman
Lesser Officers: Lieutenant Colonel, Commander, Major, Captain, Lieutenant and Ensign, Warrant Officer	Chief, Professionals (Doctors, Lawyers), Executive, Assistant to President, Executive Manager
Top Enlisted NCOs: Master Sergeant, Gunnery Sergeant, Petty Officers, Specialists, etc.	Superintendent, Foreman, Shop Chief, Unit Supervisor
Lower Enlisteds: Airman, Private, Sailor, Corporal, etc.	Skilled/Unskilled Laborer, Technician, Specialist, Clerk

Figure 11-1.

This table illustrates that both officers and enlisted personnel have important, yet distinct roles in accomplishing the duties and responsibilities of military service. Just as a factory or assembly plant cannot succeed without the efforts of its skilled and unskilled laborers, foremen, and superintendents, the military's success likewise depends on the dedication and work of its many enlisted personnel. Chiefs need braves; therefore, in the military services, there are approximately eight times as many enlisted personnel assigned as there are officers.

Both officers and enlisted personnel contribute to the vital mission of providing for the defense of our country. Indeed, this is a mission that can be achieved only with the cooperation and efficiency of servicepeople at all levels of military rank and grade.

WHY TWO SEPARATE GROUPS?

Even though officers receive more intense training than enlisteds and hold higher-level positions, the question still remains: why two separate and distinct groups? "After all," an outsider may ask, "isn't it true that, in the military, rank is rank, that an enlisted person who outranks another is still according to military regulation, in charge?" The senior person's instructions must be obeyed by the junior, even though both are enlisted. In addition, they point out that intensified management training is increasingly being provided to senior enlisted personnel. So why have a *separate* officers' grouping? Why not simply have rank without any O and E grades?

Military Combat Demands

The services believe that a separation of the two groups is necessary because of the unique combat mission of the armed forces. To be more specific, the distinction between the officer and enlisted exists, they explain, because of the demand in wartime for a military force fully trained to obey orders unquestioningly and without fail. The military law, as set forth by Congress and the President, makes disobedience of orders one of the worst offenses a serviceperson can commit; and military necessity is given as the reason for this. It is thought that a rigid hierarchical personnel system will foster and promote this unhesitating obedience.

Officer trainees and cadets are advised that they cannot be "one of the boys"; instead, they must remain aloof and distant. Thus, when the whistle blows and the officer must direct the enlisted person in battle, there will be no cries or protests of favoritism. Also, because the officer is separate and distinct from his enlisted subordinates, he can be better adapted to giving orders which, in effect, may result in death or injury. No one, it is contended, would order a friend or even a close associate into a hostile area or battle situation which could result in the friend's death. Impersonal and impartial actions, it is claimed, result in better, more decisive combat decisions.

To some, this makes sense even from the standpoint of the enlisted person. If, for example, a person is ordered into a dangerous situation by a friend, that person can certainly be expected to question the order if he deems it unwise or faulty. After all, a friend wouldn't object to being questioned, right? But in the stress and crisis of battle, when every second counts, failure to promptly carry out an order might be disastrous, particularly when the officer is expected to be more knowledgeable of the battle situation than are his enlisted personnel.

This is why, in the military units where combat skills are emphasized, one is more likely to observe a well-defined gap between the officer and the enlisted. Strict obedience to orders is demanded and much attention is paid to rank and privilege. Yet in such units (for example, the Army's Green Berets, Rangers, Airborne, and most Marine combat units), assigned personnel are often so well-trained and so highly motivated that there exists little animosity or resentment about class differences.

In point of fact, the officers, senior enlisted, and lower-ranking enlisted personnel all must endure the same privations and sacrifices demanded by combat and the preparation for battle. Because of the need for coordinated teamwork and *esprit de corps*, differences in rank and status are often blurred and become insignificant.

But even in non-combat, support units, enlisted personnel are treated as professionals in today's military services. And, indeed, they are professionals. Among their enlisted ranks, the services have not only foot soldiers and cooks, but electronics technicians, computer programmers, and air traffic controllers. But combat foot soldiers, cooks, and ordinary seamen can be just as professional in their work, demeanor, and bearing. The wise officer understands this and makes no bones about it to his subordinates. This is a far cry from the rigid caste system of the military typical in decades past, and it is indicative of a recent trend in the services toward greater equality.

The services contend that obedience to orders, as well as the show of respect due superiors, contributes to good morale, order, and discipline, elements essential to combat effectiveness. And, in fairness to the services, these guidelines apply to all military personnel, officer and enlisted. Officers are also expected to strictly obey the orders given them by higher-ranking officers.

Some enlisted personnel complain that the military system puts officers at the top of a rigid class or caste system. There probably is some truth to this, but, again, the division between officers and enlisted personnel is necessary to carry out the military's vital role of defending our nation. And, in fact, today every military force in the world, in communist, authoritarian, and free democratic countries alike, makes a distinction between officers and enlisteds.

However, unlike the situation in the armed forces of most countries around the world, every American citizen can aspire to becoming an officer. You don't have to "know someone," pay a bribe, or be of upper-class social origin. All that's necessary is that you have the ability and the desire. How to become an officer is what we'll discuss next.

12. Becoming An Officer

The U.S. military officer has the enviable position of being in one of the most respected professions in America. A Gallup Poll conducted in 1980 found that of all professions, the American public held that of military officer to be at the top in terms of respect, trust, and efficiency. The military officer was rated above the clergyman, Supreme Court Justice, doctor, and attorney.

The award of a commission as an officer in one of the five branches of the military could be one of the finest moments in your life. The commission is given by the President of the United States, with the approval of Congress. With its acceptance and after taking an oath of office, the new officer takes his place among the leaders of American society.

The value of an officer's commission cannot be overemphasized. If you don't believe it, listen to the comments of some leaders of civilian industry when asked what they think of the abilities and employment promise of former military officers:

> More often than not, the former military or naval officer brings to a civilian career important leadership qualities, an awareness of the importance of teamwork, an organizational ability and self-discipline . . .
>
> —C. H. Anderson,
> Director, Personnel Relations
> Ford Motor Company

> To ensure that our businesses are capably managed, we constantly look for leadership talent which has the alertness and ability to anticipate and adjust with change. One important source of such management talent is the college graduate who has enriched his academic credentials with practical 'real time' decision-making experience in the military services.
>
> —J. Peter Grace, President
> W.R. Grace & Company

> We have been extremely pleased with the performance of college graduates who have come to us following active military duty. . . . These young men and women have developed a level of maturity that places them in a position to assume greater responsibility than their contemporaries . . .
>
> —J. E. Lander, Vice President
> Conoco Oil Company

> ITT (is) keenly aware of the qualities of leadership, maturity, and responsibility developed through service in the U.S. military.
>
> —Francis J. Dunleavy
> Vice Chairman
> International Telephone and Telegraph Company

THE
PRESIDENT
OF
THE UNITED STATES OF AMERICA

To all who shall see these presents, greeting:

Know ye, that reposing special trust and confidence in the patriotism, valor, fidelity and abilities of   JOHN DOE   *, I do appoint*   HIM   SECOND LIEUTENANT   *in the*

United States Air Force

to   DATE   *as such from the*   TWENTY-SIXTH   *day of*   JANUARY   *, nineteen hundred and*   EIGHTY-THREE   *This officer will therefore carefully and diligently discharge the duties of the office to which appointed by doing and performing all manner of things thereunto belonging.*

And I do strictly charge and require those officers and other personnel of lesser rank to render such obedience as is due an officer of this grade and position. And this officer is to observe and follow such orders and directions, from time to time, as may be given by the President of the United States of America, or other superior officers acting in accordance with the laws of the United States of America.

This commission is to continue in force during the pleasure of the President of the United States of America, under the provisions of those public laws relating to **Officers of the Armed Forces of the United States of America** *and the component thereof in which this appointment is made.*

Done at the City of Washington, this   TWENTY-SIXTH   *day of*   JANUARY *in the year of our Lord, one thousand nine hundred and*   EIGHTY-THREE   *, and of the Independence of the United States of America, the*   TWENTY-SIXTH.

By the President:

Lieutenant General, USAF
Deputy Chief of Staff,
Manpower and Personnel

Secretary of the Air Force

Figure 12-1.

Through experience we have found that self-discipline and dedication to achievement that normally characterize a successful military officer are the same qualities which make the person an excellent candidate for employment with Firestone.

—Richard A. Riley
Chairman & Chief Executive Officer
Firestone Tire & Rubber Company

Military experience and leadership training is readily transferable to the management skills that are most in demand in business.

—Harry Holiday, Jr.
President, Armco Steel Corporation

PATHWAYS TO A COMMISSION

There are several paths you can take to earn an officer's commission. The one standing requirement of all the services' officer's programs, however, is that only college graduates be commissioned. An exception is the Army.

The Army has two programs for non-college graduates. First, there is the warrant officer program, which allows highly qualified non-college graduates to apply for pilot training, usually as a helicopter pilot. A second opportunity exists only for active-duty enlisted personnel and warrant officers with at least two years of college. This program is covered later in this chapter. Except for these two limited programs, Army officers come from the ranks of college graduates.

The several ways of becoming an officer are outlined below.

THE SERVICE ACADEMIES

The U.S. military academies offer the finest college education in the world. The services spend over $100,000 on each graduate. Graduates of the service academies are highly esteemed, both in American society and within the service.

There are four service academies: U.S. Military Academy at West Point, New York; Naval Academy at Annapolis, Maryland; Air Force Academy at Colorado Springs, Colorado; and Coast Guard Academy at New London, Connecticut.

The Naval Academy furnishes officers for both the Navy and the Marine Corps.

Eligibility

The admission standards for any of the service academies are high, and only high school students with exceptional grades, evidence of extracurricular activities, high motivation, and those in excellent physical condition have a chance to be accepted.

Nominations

Applicants for the U.S. military, naval, and Air Force academies must be nominated by a member of Congress or qualify under other special criteria. Appointments to the Coast Guard Academy are made competitively on a nationwide basis. If you are interested in a congressional nomination, write directly to your congressman in Washington, D.C., for more information. For application forms, college catalogs, and other information, write to the following sources:

Director of Cadet Admissions
U.S. Air Force Academy
Colorado Springs, CO 80840

Office of Admission
U.S. Military Academy
West Point, NY 10996

Office of Admissions
U.S. Coast Guard Academy
New London, CT 06320

Director of Candidate Guidance
U.S. Naval Academy
Annapolis, MD 21402

If You Aren't Accepted

If you apply to an academy and are not accepted, don't feel bad. It is easier to win admittance to prestigious schools like Yale and Harvard than to a service academy. Don't give up hope, though. There are a certain number of slots allocated for active-duty enlisted personnel in all the services. You may wish to enlist and seek admittance after proving your worth on active duty.

Also, some slots are reserved for cadets in the Reserve Officer Training Corps (ROTC) at colleges and universities around the nation.

ROTC

Want the services to pay for your college education and give you a tax-free allowance of $100 a month to boot? That's what ROTC offers through its scholarship programs.

ROTC scholarships are offered on a competitive basis and should be applied for early in your senior year of high school. If you are not tendered a full, four-year scholarship, you can enter college on your own, join the ROTC program, and apply later for a two-, three-, or three-and-a-half-year scholarship.

ROTC cadets go to college and attend classes like any other student, but they take at least one course (perhaps requiring about five hours of time per week) in military science in addition to their normal classwork. At some time in their college curriculum, the cadet will have to attend a summer training program, or programs, to help prepare him for active duty.

All ROTC cadets are paid $100 per month tax-free during their final two years in the program. In addition, Army cadets may join the active reserves. This can substantially boost the amount of money you use to defray college expenses. Also, reserve time counts for pay once the cadet graduates and enters the Army on active duty as an officer.

Air Force ROTC is offered at 146 colleges and universities; Army ROTC at 279 schools; and Navy/Marine Corps ROTC at 55. Some schools offer only a two-year program; most have both a two- and a four-year program.

Eligibility

Each service has its own admission standards. Generally, if you are admitted to the university as a student and can pass a service physical, you can enter the ROTC program. However, there may be some limitation as concerns the college majors that are acceptable. Also, you may have to maintain a minimum grade-point average and make an acceptable score on the service's officer qualification tests, as well as the Scholastic Aptitude Test (SAT) or its equivalent, the American College Testing (ACT) exam.

For more information and a scholarship application package, write to:

AFROTC Information
Maxwell AFB, AL 36112

Army ROTC
Fort Monroe, VA 23651

Commandant of the Marine Corps
HQ Marine Corps
Washington, DC 20380

NROTC
Navy Recruiting Command
401 S. Wilson Boulevard
Arlington, VA 22203

OFFICER CANDIDATE/TRAINING SCHOOLS

Another, more direct way to gain an officer's commission is for a college graduate to seek acceptance to one of the services' in-house officer training programs. These are:

Air Force Officer Training School (OTS).   Twelve weeks long (15 for pilot candidates who do not possess a private pilot license). Students are placed on active duty in the rank of staff sergeant and are commissioned as second lieutenants

(O-1) upon graduation. They then proceed to active duty or on to a training school (for instance, pilot or navigator training).

Army Officer Candidate Course (OCC). Fourteen weeks long. The OCC is open not only to graduates of accredited civilian colleges who first enlist in the reserve Army, but also to enlisted personnel and warrant officers who possess as little as a two-year college equivalency.

Coast Guard Officer Candidate School (OCS). Seventeen weeks long. For graduates of accredited colleges and universities.

Marine Corps Officer Candidate Class and Aviation Officer Candidate School. Ten weeks long; however, enlisted personnel must then attend a 21-week basic school. Aviation officers receive additional training for 12 to 18 months to earn their wings.

Marine Platoon Leaders Class (PLC). This program is akin to the ROTC opportunity. College freshmen, sophomores, and juniors at accredited colleges attend two six-week sessions or one ten-week session during summer vacation(s) at a Marine school in Quantico, Virginia. Students in the PLC receive $100 a month financial aid. After college graduation, they must complete the 21-week basic school.

Navy Officer Candidate School (OCS). Sixteen weeks long. For graduates of accredited colleges and universities. Leads to commissioning as an ensign (O-1).

Naval Aviation Officer Candidate School. After 15 weeks, the cadet is commissioned as an ensign (O-1). He then proceeds to aviation school, which takes about 15 months and earns the officer his wings.

For information on any of the services' officer candidate training schools, call the local military recruiter.

DIRECT APPOINTMENTS

Direct appointments are available to highly qualified professionals in medical and allied health fields, lawyers, and chaplains. Students in the fields of law and medicine, including those in programs leading to certification as a registered nurse, dietician, physical therapist, and physician, should inquire about financial assistance from the services. Keep in mind, however, that the military doesn't provide this aid without obligation; a commitment of several years may be required. Contact the local military recruiter for details.

13. Pay And Benefits

Your love gives me such a thrill,
but your love don't pay my bills . . .
I need money.

—Rock song from the 50s

Everyone is interested in how much money a job pays, and, increasingly, workers are becoming concerned about the fringe benefits a firm or company offers its employees. Now, pay and benefits may not be *the* most important consideration for you in whether or not you find a certain job attractive; perhaps patriotism and idealism, job satisfaction, adventure, travel, variety, or other factors also excite your interest. Nevertheless, everyone needs money to live, and civilian enterprises like to pride themselves on how well they are able to compensate their employees.

MILITARY PAY . . . IT'S NOT BAD!

Way back in 1881, a private in the Army was paid the paltry sum of $13 a month. The pay of an average civilian factory worker at the time was about four times that amount. By the time World War II rolled around, in 1941, the beginning pay for a draftee was an unspectacular $21 a month. This was far off the pace of his civilian counterpart, whose median salary, according to the Labor Department, averaged $320 per month.

Things began to brighten financially for the people in uniform in the 1950s and 1960s, and particularly in the 1970s, with the advent of the all-volunteer military. To attract and keep quality personnel, the government recognized that it was necessary to raise military pay so that it would be comparable with that of civilian workers, so the pay scales were adjusted upward.

Today, military pay and benefits are considered by many experts, both in and out of service, to be the equal of that obtainable in civilian jobs. Naturally, this varies depending on which civilian career field one chooses. The military does not pay by career field but, instead, by the rank or military grade of an individual. This means that an E-7 (master sergeant) cook in the Air Force will be paid much more than, say, an E-2 (airman) computer programmer. This is far different from civilian life, where pay varies according to the type of work performed.

WHO SETS PAY RATES?

Congress and the President decide how much pay, as well as what fringe benefits, servicepeople receive. Typically, a pay raise is given the services at the beginning of each fiscal year (October 1). Sometimes, the pay increase is a large one, equalling or greater than the cost-of-living increase for the period, and sometimes it is less. Naturally, unless military pay is permitted to keep up with the inflation rate, servicepeople lose purchasing power because their dollars will buy less and less.

Usually, if military pay has not been adjusted to keep up with inflation, it begins to lag behind civilian pay levels and servicepeople become disgruntled and unhappy. As a result, many leave the service for "greener pastures,"—that is, higher paying jobs. If too many people leave, Congress and the President become alarmed and they vote to raise military pay to bring it into line with that given to civilians.

People in uniform have no union and few powerful lobbying groups to represent them, and so the issue of military pay and benefits—whether to provide or increase—is left up to the will (some claim the caprice) of the politicians in Washington.

But Congress has generally displayed a sense of fairness in determining pay scales and pay raises for the military. Some congressmen fear that if military pay does not keep up with that of civilians, a severe manpower drain will occur and experienced personnel will be lost. Also, Congress knows that inadequate pay makes recruiting a next-to-impossible task.

COMPARISON WITH CIVILIAN PAY

The military has not fared badly in recent years in regard to pay and benefits. In fact, according to many studies, military compensation compares very favorably with that received by civilian workers.

Many compensation experts say that, for a woman, military pay is far greater than one can expect in the civilian workplace. And for a young man *or* woman in the 17–21-year age category, the financial rewards of military service are rosy indeed. A Department of Defense study in 1982 found that total military compensation (actual dollars received) for young people in this age bracket was *23 percent higher* for service personnel.

For college graduates, the attractiveness of military pay is also a real inducement to sign up at the recruiter's office. Except for a select few individuals graduating with majors in high demand by civilian employers—mainly engineers and scientists—the military has much more to offer financially. If the graduate's major is in the social sciences or liberal arts areas, his starting pay in uniform, according to Department of Labor sources, will be as much as fifty percent more than he would get as a civilian worker.

THE TYPES OF MILITARY PAY

Military pay is unlike that of civilians. Why? Well, simply because servicepeople do not receive a salary as such. Instead, their pay comes in several different packages. First is base pay. This constitutes the largest part of your pay while in uniform.

In addition to base pay, you may also receive bonuses and other allowances. The two most important are housing (called the quarters allowance) and food (officially called basic allowance for subsistence, or BAS). Since the general words *housing* and *food* are easier to digest mentally, those are the terms we'll use in this book.

There are also several other allowances, such as foreign service pay, clothing maintenance allowance, flight pay, hazardous duty pay, overseas incentive pay, divers' pay, and hostile fire pay. In addition, you might be eligible for an enlistment or reenlistment bonus. Not everyone is eligible for these special payments.

(As we discuss military pay and benefits, you should keep in mind that all the figures in this chapter are based on the pay scales and public laws in effect as of the year this book was written, 1982. Military compensation is subject to continuous change. A recruiter can give you current data.)

Base Pay

All servicepeople are given base pay in an amount which depends on their rank. A general, quite obviously, will receive a good deal more than a young airman or seaman. Also, base pay increases with seniority—the number of years you stay in the service. For instance, as of October 1981, an airman first class (E-1) with under two years of service received $642.60 per month. After two years, that would increase to $677.00, and after four years, $705 as base pay.

Base pay is taxable income and you will be docked for income tax as well as Social Security deductions just like civilian pay. But the other major components of your pay, housing and food, are nontaxable. You will receive in your pay the full amount of these allowances. No deductions are made at all. This means *more money in your pocket!*

Housing Allowance

All service members receive either a housing allowance or free housing. Again, the amount depends on your rank. A young soldier just coming on active duty gets $118 a month. A top-ranking sergeant would pull down much more, about $262. On the other hand, a four-star general can expect to receive $489 for a housing allowance.

The amount of your housing allowance also depends on whether or not you have dependents—a spouse, children, or perhaps a mother who depends on you for over fifty percent of her support. Personnel who have dependents are given larger housing payments.

For example, take the case of two airmen first class (A1C): one single, one married. The single A1C receives $141 per month as a housing allowance, whereas the married A1C, because he has dependents, would take in $206 per month, $45 more. Single military personnel often scream that this is discriminatory and that it violates the principle of "equal pay for equal work"—and it does. But this is the system Congress has prescribed. Not surprisingly, married servicepeople rarely object or complain about the inequity.

If You Live on Post

If you live on a military station, you will *not* receive a housing allowance. Instead, you will be allowed to live rent-free. This is true for either married persons who reside with their families in military housing or single people who live in a military dormitory or barracks.

In this situation, the military feels it is providing you housing quarters for which you pay neither rent, taxes, nor utilities, so a housing allowance is not justified.

Variable Housing Allowance

Recently, Congress approved the payment of a variable housing allowance (VHA) for service personnel in the United States. This is only paid to those who live off the military installation. The VHA is designed to defray the extraordinary housing costs some people have because they live in a high-cost living area. This is why the payment is called a *variable* housing allowance. Its amount varies according to *where* you live. If you live in Wyoming or Kansas, both areas where housing costs are relatively low, your VHA payment may be only a few dollars a month, or nothing. On the other hand, living off base in an expensive locale like Washington, D.C., for Los Angeles might net you more than $100 per month.

Food Allowance

Can you feed yourself and your family, if married, on $4.50 per day? Maybe not, but that's what the service will give you, an enlisted person, for a food allowance. That translates to $135 per month, tax-free. Interestingly, due to a quirk in the law, officers get less than enlisted members, receiving only $94 per month.

Not Everyone Gets It

If you are a single enlisted person and you are required to live on post (most new servicepeople are), you will not be given a food allowance. Instead, you will be given a meal card which entitles you to eat for free in your post's military dining hall. If you decide to eat elsewhere, fine, but you still won't get an allowance or be paid for the meals you pass up at the dining hall.

Predictably, many single enlisted persons complain that this policy is unfair and discriminatory. "Why," they ask, "should all the officers and married enlisted personnel be given cash in the form of a food allowance and spend the money any way and anywhere they want, while the single enlisteds are forced to eat at the dining hall?" Good question.

The answer lies in military manpower needs, economics, and the budget. The military has spent millions of dollars building dining halls and has staffed them with both civilian and military cooks and food service employees. This is a large investment. To pay single enlisteds to eat anywhere they choose may mean that many, if not most, of these military dining halls would have to be closed. Military cooks would have to be retrained into other career fields.

If war was to break out in some distant corner of the globe, military cooks and food service personnel would be needed, and they might not be available. Napoleon once said "An army travels on its stomach," meaning that sustenance is vital to the morale of the troops. For this reason, and because of the investment already incurred, single enlisteds are encouraged, by issuance of meal cards, to use the dining hall—and they are not paid a food allowance.

Of course, when you are overseas or in a remote location of the United States where there are no civilian eating establishments, this whole issue is moot. The military dining hall is then the "only place in town."

Other Allowances and Pay

As mentioned earlier, in addition to base pay and allowances for housing and food, there are several other special allowances and payments which many servicepeople receive. As a matter of fact, there are so many different pays and special allowances that it boggles the mind. Even seasoned military personnel are often confused by the diversity of payments in the military compensation system. It's a virtual "octopus" apparatus, meaning that there are payments wrapped around other payments.

It is best to keep in mind, when reading of the various ways in which military people get paid, that very few persons get more than a few of these special payments. What you can count on, however, is base pay (which everyone gets), food, and housing allowances—which everyone either receives in cash or in "kind" (free meals or housing on the post).

As for special pays and allowances to be discussed, whether or not you will receive one or more depends on such factors as the specific job specialty you perform and the geographic area to which you are assigned. With that in mind, let's examine these special, or supplemental, payments.

Flight Pay

Officers and enlisted personnel whose primary duty is flying in a plane receive flight pay. How much flight pay you get depends on your military rank. Officers can receive up to $400 a month, enlisted personnel as much as $131. You don't have to be a pilot to be eligible for flight pay. If you have any job which regularly requires you to fly as a crew member (navigator, gunner, radar technician, or loading specialist), you are authorized this special pay.

Hazardous Duty Pay

Do you have the inclination to work with dangerous explosives or to be a parachutist or paratrooper? If you do, and the services use your skills in a hazardous duty job, you will receive $83 a month extra if you are enlisted, $110 if an officer.

Diving Pay

Navy frogmen and others who dive underwater as a part of their jobs are recipients of a stipend of $300 if enlisted, and $200 if an officer.

Foreign Service Pay

There you are in your Army uniform in a biting sandstorm. No trees in sight, just a few camels and women with covered faces. This isn't "Mecca," that's for sure, but it is an assignment that can net you several extra bucks in pay. Foreign service pay ranges from $8.00 to $22.50 per month, depending on the degree of austerity and the isolation of the foreign location. Being assigned to London, England, or Munich, West Germany, won't get you this pay. Living for a year or two in a tough place like Tin City, Alaska (way up north) or in an Egyptian desert will.

Sea Pay

Sailors assigned shipboard duty receive extra money each month, according to their rank. For instance, a person with three years of service may receive about $405 *extra* per month.

Submarine Pay

Join a submarine crew and, in addition to sea pay, the Navy will give you another $100 per month. Hanging out in deep waters with the fish and sharks may just be worthwhile, after all—unless, of course, you are prone to attacks of claustrophobia, the fear of being in tight or small spaces.

Hostile Fire Pay

This is more commonly called combat pay. It is aid to military personnel who are assigned to areas of conflict where they might be fired on by an enemy. It seems unusual to pay servicepeople extra for what some feel is merely part of the normal duties and risks of military life, but Congress has deemed it only fair to pay soldiers, airmen, sailors, and Marines under hostile fire $65 per month more than servicepeople not involved in the conflict. It's hard to deny that men in combat, risking their lives and fighting for our country, deserve this supplemental payment.

After all, how many civilians would brave enemy machine guns and tanks for the relatively paltry sum of $65 each month?

Special Payment for Overseas Living

If you are assigned to a high-cost area overseas, you may receive allowances to enable you to at least maintain American living standards. When one considers that steak in Tokyo, Japan, can cost $20 a pound and that the annual premium for auto insurance in West Germany can go as high as $1,200 per year, it becomes understandable why personnel living in these areas need supplemental income.

Proficiency Pay

Enlisted and officer personnel in a few career fields receive proficiency pay. This is a payment of up to $150 given to personnel in critical career areas. Its purpose is to induce trained and experienced personnel in technical fields to stay in the service. In effect, it's a morale-booster payment. Its message to people with marketable skills such as electronics and mechanical engineering is "Don't leave the service for a lucrative and tempting position with a civilian firm. We care!" The fact that a goodly number of critically needed people do opt to leave the services each year is the reason why proficiency pay is continued.

Clothing Allowance

Initially, the service will provide you with a complete set of uniforms. You'll be outfitted with everything you need to get started in military life. After this initial uniform issue, you will have to buy your own clothing and accessories. And you are, of course, responsible for maintaining your uniforms, having them cleaned and serviced.

To help out enlisted personnel with this expense, a clothing allowance is given. This allowance isn't much—about $6 to $12 per month, depending on the service—but it does help a bit to soften the blow of having to buy uniforms when your first set begins to wear.

A clothing allowance for officers? Sorry, but evidently it's felt that the officers are paid well enough to take care of this expense themselves. Officers are, of course, furnished with their first set of uniforms. After that, they're on their own.

Bonuses

Want up to $5,000 cash quickly? That's what the services offer qualified persons under a unique bonus program. Bonuses may be paid to certain new recruits shortly after they enlist, and to personnel in critical career fields, and combat specialties who agree to re-enlist.

Enlistment Bonus

The enlistment bonus is usually paid only to a person who agrees to enlist for more than a minimum number of years in either a combat or a critical career field. As the needs of the service change, the amount of the bonus and the affected career fields vary greatly.

As of 1982, all the services except the Air Force paid an enlistment bonus. The Army is most generous. It offers bonuses of $500 to $5,000 to applicants who can qualify for fields such as intelligence, languages, combat infantry, and electronics. The Navy tenders up to $2,000 for enlistees who qualify for specialties like communications, boiler technician, sonar technician, radar repairers, and gunner's mate. The recruiters can tell you what career fields now qualify, what the required length of service commitment is, and how much the bonus will be.

If your interest is aroused and you think you might qualify, look into these programs. It could mean a lot of money for you—right up front—as soon as you enlist and complete your training.

A word of caution, however. As we mentioned, to get this bonus you will have to agree to stay in service for a longer period of time than the typical recruit, and the training for a specific career field may be both long and arduous. Some of the Navy's schools for qualifying specialties are up to a year and longer in duration and you might have to contract for an initial enlistment of up to six years of active duty.

The lengthy training period would seem valuable and worthwhile; it certainly is not a bad thing to receive free training in a complex (and marketable) skill. But the military's technical schools can be quite demanding, so make sure you have the requisite dedication and drive *before* you sign up for one of these fields.

Reenlistment Bonus

You're nearing the end of your initial tour of duty. Whew!! Those four years have been so long. "I can't wait," you say, "until I get that hard-earned discharge."

"Hey, Bob," says your friendly personnel specialist, "did you know the Navy will give you $20,000 to re-enlist for another six years?"

"What? $20,000?" you exclaim. "Where are the papers? Let me sign 'em!"

That story isn't real, but huge re-enlistment bonuses aren't fables. All the services pay people in certain critically needed career fields a large sum of money, up to $20,000. Usually the fields are those in which civilian job recruiters are trying to lure trained military personnel. The majority are highly technical, but this isn't always the case. Re-enlisting in some fields will get you this maximum payment; some will enable you to receive less. *Most* career fields pay none.

As is the case with almost all special pay, all this is subject to change, and even if you enter the service in one of these high-paying re-enlistment fields, by the time you become eligible for re-enlistment, your field may no longer be eligible for a large bonus or even *any* bonus.

Officer Bonus

You could probably use $15,000, couldn't you? Most of us could. Well, if you are a qualified officer, you might be able to receive an initial bonus in this amount for volunteering for fields such as medicine, submarine engineering, nuclear engineering, and a few others. Naturally, to qualify, you will have to meet the educational prerequisites.

For instance, the medical bonus is paid *only* to licensed physicians, and to enter the nuclear engineering field you would have to possess an appropriate college degree.

Some officers in highly technical and undermanned fields also receive bonuses when they agree to stay past their initial period of obligated active duty.

The Military "Salary"

All these components, then—bonuses, special pay, allowances, base pay, housing, and food allowances—make up the "salary" of the serviceperson. Twice each month, on the 15th and on the last day of the month, you will receive a single paycheck that combines all the payments for which you are eligible. The military does not call it a salary, but, in effect, that's what it is. It is the direct pay you will receive as compensation for your services in support of your nation's defense.

However, direct pay is not the only means of rewarding people for their contributions and dedication in performing work tasks and duties. The fringe benefits offered are often just as important for a person as how many dollars of take-home pay are earned. Anyone who objectively analyzes the nature of the fringe benefits the military offers its people would have to conclude that they are second to none.

Fringe Benefits

Today, the level of fringe benefits is considered a significant way to measure how much one gets in real or "total," compensation. Corporations like Exxon, IBM, and General Motors report that up to one-third of their labor costs result from an accumulation of fringe benefits afforded employees. These "fringies," as they are called, can add up to thousands of dollars for each worker in indirect compensation. They include contributions in retirement or pension funds, medical and dental insurance policies, Social Security payments, stock option plans, and bonuses.

Civilian employers seem to be offering more in the way of fringe benefits with each passing year. Still, their benefits pale in comparison with the more generous fringe benefit programs provided by the military services. Let's take a look at some of the benefits a military man acquires from the first day on active duty.

Medical Care

You start your service career by receiving a complete medical exam. Only if you are in tip-top medical condition will you be allowed to enter active duty. From your first day at basic training, the serviceperson receives full and complete medical care *at no cost*.

Have a toothache? The service dentist will take care of it. Need glasses? No problem. The services have opthalmologists and optometrists. In fact, the military system of medical clinics and hospitals is so huge that hundreds of millions of dollars are spent on it each year to keep it operating. Whatever your medical problem, the military system will handle it. As a person in uniform, you are covered 100 percent, without exceptions.

This benefit extends to any dependents you have, too. Except for routine dental care, the military will foot the bill for all medical expenses. If it is necessary for your dependents to seek medical attention from a civilian physician or medical facility, the service will reimburse you for up to 80 percent of the cost.

Of course, the worth of any medical benefit depends on how much you use it. But consider the incredible cost of medical assistance. In the unfortunate circumstance that you or your dependents need major medical attention, perhaps due to injuries sustained as a result of an accident, or a life-threatening illness, you are protected.

Some people in civilian life have literally gone bankrupt by the necessity to pay thousands of dollars in medical bills. Not so for the military person and his dependents (if any). In fact, the hospitalized serviceperson is covered even if the injury occurs off the military installation. In such a case, all that's necessary is for the serviceperson to show the hospital the military I.D. card. It's accepted everywhere as proof that, eventually, Uncle Sam will reimburse the doctor, clinic, and/or hospital for services provided.

One other point should be considered. Unlike many civilian jobs, when you are ill and miss work in the service your full pay and status continues. This is true even if you are hospitalized for an extended period of time. And if it is necessary to discharge you for medical reasons, the Veteran's Administration will pay you benefits as a civilian for service-connected disabilities.

What is this medical benefit worth to you? A comparable insurance plan in the civil service would cost a person about $35 per month, and a family about $70. But the civil service insurance is cheaper because it is a group plan covering thousands of civilian government employees. The premiums for comparable medical insurance coverage for most civilian workers would set you back anywhere from $75 to $200 a month, depending on the insurer and the size of the group covered.

Looking at this military benefit on an annual basis, and comparing it to what's available from civilian insurance plans, we can see that it can be worth at least $420 per year and as much as $2,400.

Life Insurance Programs

Naturally you are young, hopefully healthy, and don't expect to "kick the bucket" soon. Still, all of us have to go some time and, believe it or not, you are not exempt! So, assuming the worst does occur, how does the service provide for its departed members?

If you die on active duty, your survivors are eligible for life insurance and other payments. By special arrangement with civilian life insurers, the military services offer their members up to $35,000 of life insurance at only about one-fourth of the cost civilians would have to pay. In addition, the government would award your beneficiaries a $3,000 death gratuity. Plus, your dependents would receive monthly assistance payments ranging from $415 to $567 a month, depending on your rank. All in all, the Department of Defense has calculated a civilian would have to pay about $40 per month for the coverage that the service person gets for free.

Social Security

While in the military, you are eligible for old-age retirement and disability benefits on the same basis as civilians. But, just like civilians, you'll have to make the required payments to the Social Security system. In 1982, this amounted to 6.65 percent of basic pay. However, the part of your total pay that comes from allowances—housing and food—is *not taxable*. This is another benefit for you as it means you can pocket the 6.65 percent you otherwise would have to cough up for Social Security payment.

Retirement Pension

Okay, so retirement for you is a long way off. It's probably not an important consideration for most young people! This is one of those benefits that recruiters only touch on, if indeed they discuss retirement at all. Nevertheless, retirement benefits are something you should weigh carefully when seeking a job position, whether as a civilian or in the military. Someday, you'll be glad you did. As you grow older, thoughts of retirement, and especially the problem of how to provide for yourself financially while in retirement, will take on more and more significance.

The military retirement program is often called the jewel of military fringe benefits. It is the envy of most civilians and is highly acknowledged to be one of the best, if not *the* best, pension plan in existence anywhere—at least for the average American.

The retirement plan of the services is so lucrative that it has become a constant source of congressional debate. Many congressmen claim it is excessive and way too expensive. While they debate, though, thousands of servicepeople quit each year with a guaranteed monthly income and several added benefits, as discussed below.

Comparison with Civilian Plans

Just how great is the military retirement system in comparison with other plans? The Congressional Budget Office recently conducted a study that contrasted the total dollar value of a typical enlistee's retirement and the value of retirement from other jobs. Here are the results.

Military Enlistee	$280,000
Policeman	95,000
Fireman	95,000
Federal Civil Service	26,000
Private Company	14,000

The figures above show that the serviceperson would get almost three times as much in retirement benefits as a police officer or fire fighter, and 20 times as much as the average worker in civilian industry!

How it Works

You can spend as few as 20 years in the service and retire with a sizeable pension for the rest of your life. Now, 20 years may sound like forever if you're, say, 18 or 21 years old, but consider this: if you join the service at age 18, you would be eligible to retire 20 years later, at the age of 38. Even the most generous civilian pension plans target the mid- to late 50s as the earliest a person can retire. Most, however, require employees to work to age 62 or 65.

In the military, you can retire anytime after 20 years of service. At that point, the government would reward you with 50 percent of the base pay you were earning just prior to retirement. However, for each additional year past 20, you will get an added two and a half percent of your base pay. Let's take an example. Say you retire as a chief master sergeant in the Air Force:

- If you retire after 20 years of service, you would get about $930 per month for the rest of your life.

- After 25 years of service, it would increase to $1,163 per month.

- After 30 years, your monthly retirement check would total $1,395.

Now, let's observe how an officer may fare when he retires. The average officer calls it quits at the rank of lieutenant colonel. If you stay in the service for a career, you may achieve even higher rank.

- After 20 years of service—$1,530

- After 25 years of service—$1,913

- After 30 years of service—$2,295

Retirement may indeed be a long way off, but wouldn't it be nice, at the early age of 38 or 42, to see a check come in the mail every month in the amount of $900, $1,500, or even $3,000.

Your Contribution

Virtually every other retirement plan, whether government or private, requires that the individual contribute toward his retirement. For example, in civil service you would have to contribute seven percent of your gross pay to a retirement fund. The pension plans of corporations like IBM, U.S. Steel, and others have similar provisions.

How much do you personally contribute toward military retirement? Nothing, not one cent. It is entirely free. What this means, in effect, is that your paycheck ultimately is *at least* about seven percent or even higher than it otherwise would be. Whereas most plans "giveth, then taketh away," the military system just takes care of the whole "shebang." No wonder that so many civilians are envious of military retirees.

Cut-rate Groceries

One of the best ways for servicepeople to stretch their dollars is to shop at the commissary. The commissary is the military equivalent of a supermarket. Located on military installations, they offer groceries, meat, produce, and other items at incredibly low prices. In fact, the prices at the commissary are at wholesale levels.

The commissary system is larger than any supermarket chain in the country. Only military personnel and their immediate families can shop in commissaries.

Commissaries are run by the services as non-profit ventures. How much money you can save by shopping at the commissary depends, of course, on the size of your family. But studies have shown that the average saving is about 29 percent as compared to outside food chains.

Leave/Vacation Time

All servicepeople are given 30 days of leave each year (two and half days per month). Your first leave will probably start after basic training, or soon afterward. Leave is the equivalent of vacation time for civilians.

The 30-day period covers both weekends and holidays as well as weekdays, so the total time available to you may actually not be a full 30 "work" days, but as few as 20. In other words, if you fly from your base in San Antonio on Saturday to your civilian home in Topeka, Kansas, and stay for nine straight days before returning, you will be charged with nine days leave even though your normal duty week is from Monday to Friday. In this example, the two weekends (4 days) count as leave time taken.

However, many servicepeople take short leaves of five days, from Monday through Friday, so that days on weekends won't count as chargeable leave. In that instance, the individual *can* take a full 30 days of leave, five days at a time.

When you are discharged or separated from the service, you will be paid for all the leave time you have to your credit, up to 60 days.

Educational Assistance

This benefit is covered in great detail elsewhere in this book. To just summarize, military people in off-duty education programs may have 75 to 90 percent of their tuition paid by the government. Members living on a military installation who have school-age children enrolled in military elementary and secondary schools benefit because they are not required to pay either tuition or school taxes.

Some Other Benefits

Other benefits available to service personnel and worth mentioning are described on the next page.

Legal Counseling

Military lawyers provide free legal assistance. This is a limited service, but valuable nonetheless. Need a will, a power of attorney, or a document notarized? You can have it done at no cost. Also, military lawyers can advise (but not represent) you in civilian court cases and litigation.

Travel on Military Aircraft

Every year, thousands of servicepeople fly free of charge on Air Force planes, on a space-available basis. You can't make a reservation; it's sort of a stand-by system. How does Bermuda, London, New York, or Greece sound? A free military "hop" could get you there.

Athletic Facilities

Your own fully equipped gymnasium, including sauna or steam bath, weights, basketball, tennis, and racquet ball courts. A dream? Not for service members. Most military posts have such facilities, and they are generally yours to use at no charge.

Putting it All Together

Confused by all the various military pays and the wide range of benefits? If so, don't feel alone. Even people who work in military finance and accounting offices are often bewildered by a system which provides dozens of pays and benefits. A salary system—everything in one lump sum—would be nice, but it isn't in the works.

But right now, probably the most important questions on your mind are: "What will I get paid?" "When I go to the mailbox and find my first paycheck, how much will it be?" "As time goes on, and I attain more rank and service time, how much will my pay increase?" Good questions. Let's answer them.

The average serviceperson can expect to be paid each month according to the pay scale depicted in Figure 13-1. The totals include housing and food allowances, but not other special pays and allowances. Also, the figures exclude any considerations of fringe benefits or taxes.

Note that the figures are *averages*. They assume that if you stay in the service, you will be promoted along with your contemporaries. But you might be an exception and be what is called a "fast burner"—a person whose performance shines so much that he is promoted ahead of his peers. If you are a fast burner (it takes effort!), your pay will outstrip that of the pay scale in Figure 13-1.

Also, this table doesn't take into consideration service differences. We have seen that Army personnel win more rapid promotions, followed by the Navy, Marines, and the Air Force, in that order. The reason for this variation is simple: the Army has a greater turnover of personnel.

For each high-ranking person who leaves the service, another can be promoted to take his rank and place. The more turnover of personnel departing, the more promotions. As the Air Force has the least turnover and the most favorable re-enlistment and retention rates, fewer promotion opportunities exist in that service.

MONTHLY PAY

Years of Service	Enlisted	Officer*
0 (starting out)	$ 925	$1,435
2	1,080	1,775
4	1,275	2,330
8	1,500	2,500
12	1,725	2,875
16	1,830	3,370
20	2,095	3,620
26	2,635	4,480

*Other than warrant officers

Figure 13-1

And Finally, After You're Out . . .

You'll have to admit that the pay and benefits offered by the military are actually pretty good. You won't be able to save up to buy that castle overlooking the hills of the Rhine, nor will you be able to garage two Mercedes sports cars and a Jaguar at the same time; still, you can live decently on military pay.

Now, some even better news. Someday, when you leave the military, as everyone eventually does, you'll still be drawing a few benefits and dollars. Many states have benefit programs for veterans. Some provide low-cost mortgage loans. Texas gives veterans low-interest loans to buy farmland, and other states offer bonuses. Also, there are the benefits for veterans under the programs of the federal Veterans Administration (VA).

The VA provides low-cost mortgage loans to veterans, usually below the current market interest rates. Also, when you reach the age of 65, you can use VA military hospitals. The VA also administers the Veteran's Educational Assistance Program. Under this program, the serviceperson begins an educational fund while in service. He makes a monthly payment to the fund and the government matches his contribution on a two-for-one basis. A person can invest up to $2,700 this way while in service, and the government kicks in $5,400 more, making a total of $8,100 the veteran has for college after being discharged.

However, the Army has an even better program, and only the Army has it. It's called the Army College Fund. You'll have to meet certain qualifications—like being in a certain occupational skill and scoring 50 or above on the Armed Forces Qualification Test (AFQT). If you qualify, you'll be eligible to really rake in some post-discharge college money. What you do is contribute $100 a month from your paycheck. Not only does the government match you two-for-one in your college fund, but it gives you bonuses for each year you enlist. In two years, you can accumulate $15,200 in the fund; in three years, $20,100; and in four years, $25,000! And it's all yours after you leave service. There is one stipulation, however: you must attend college or a vocational school to get it.

14. The Veteran

You've done your time. You've spent two, three, four, or maybe six years in the armed forces of the United States. Now you're an ex-GI, a veteran. The service has given you an honorable discharge certificate and you now are enjoying civilian life. "Home Air Force Base" is what airmen used to call it.

What has the service done for you? Well, it all depends on what you did for it.

- Did you seek out a career field that best used your talents? If so, then you probably have some valuable job experiences—courtesy of the military.

- Did you ask for and receive job training, both in technical schools and on the job? If so, you probably have a certificate, a diploma, or some other service document to show civilian employers that you learned a marketable skill— courtesy of the U.S. military.

- Did you voluntarily participate in off-duty education programs offered at little or no cost to you? If so, you can show a civilian employer the transcript, or you can transfer the credits to another civilian school and continue your college education—again, courtesy of the U.S. military.

Sadly, a few individuals enter the service and literally waste their time and the military's. They don't apply themselves in training, they never become fully proficient and productive in their jobs, they shirk duty, and they are quick to say, "I can't wait to leave this crummy place and go back to civilian life."

Over the years, I've seen a few of these individuals. They're miserable while they're in the service. But if you go back to before they came into the service and then track them after they leave it, chances are you'd find out that they are also miserable outside of the military. Like leopards, people don't change their spots so easily.

Undoubtedly, the fact that you cared enough to read this book puts you in a class several notches above the individuals described above. You want to make the most of your years in service and you want to get the job and training to help you progress in life and improve yourself. And, yes, you want to serve your country.

Most servicepeople fall into this category. They're above average. They—and you—are the reason why our nation has lasted over 200 years and is still the beacon of freedom in a troubled world. They—and you—are the reason why we just might be a beacon to the world 200 years from now.

Best of luck to you as you embark on an exciting and rewarding experience in the U.S. military. Some day, when you're a veteran, I believe you'll look back on your days in the military with pride and say to yourself, "It was all worth it!"

Index